PRAISE FOR
# GET ON TRACK

"Paula Dieli brings years of practical wisdom to life in *Get on Track*, leveraging her experience in successfully building Zendesk's PMO from scratch and making it a key ingredient in Zendesk's unprecedented growth and success. Paula provides deep insights and a guidebook on what any fast-growing company needs to put in place to be successful—you simply have to follow it."

**TOM KEISER**, CEO, Hootsuite

"A great program manager doesn't run boring status meetings—rather, they add real value to the business. Paula Dieli has built and scaled teams that excel at program management. *Get on Track* is an insightful reflection from all of her experience."

**AMANDA KLEHA**, Chief Customer Officer, Figma

"Paula Dieli has written a must-read primer for anyone running a fast-growing organization. Chaos and failure are too often the parents of a program management function. This delightful guide, filled with experience and best practices from a proven authority, deftly captures the essentials of PMO creation, execution, and success."

**ADRIAN MCDERMOTT**, President of Products, Zendesk

"*Get on Track* presents the qualities of program management done right. Like designing software, elegantly implementing program management processes requires skill, empathy and patience. Follow Paula Dieli's lead, and you'll be able to run your program management office with care and efficiency."

**MORTEN PRIMDAHL**, Founder, Zendesk

"I will be hoarding a stash of *Get on Track* to give to every founder and leader who asks me for advice on how to scale and execute *strategically*. Having personally experienced Paula Dieli's transformative work in building the PMO function for Zendesk, I'm grateful to see Paula share her methodology, frameworks, and best practices in such an actionable and accessible way. If you want to make your most important initiatives successful and your cross-functional teams work well together—not to mention lower your overall stress—you'll want to read and apply the lessons from this book."

**ANNE RAIMONDI**, Lecturer in Management, Stanford GSB and independent board director at Asana, Gusto, Patreon, and Guru

"*Get on Track* is a great roadmap for starting up and managing a program management team within a company. Paula Dieli's real secret sauce is the relationships she builds across an organization and within her team—and here she gives you tools on how you can also lead your organization and team to successfully complete complex projects."

**JOE FERRERO**, Director of Sales Operations, Databricks

# GET ON TRACK

# GET ON TRACK

## How to Build, Run, and Level Up Your Program Management Office

**PAULA DIELI**

Cataloguing in publication information is available from
Library and Archives Canada.
ISBN 978-1-77458-044-8 (paperback)
ISBN 978-1-77458-045-5 (ebook)

Page Two
www.pagetwo.com

Edited by Sarah Brohman
Copyedited by Crissy Calhoun
Cover and interior design by Jennifer Lum
pauladieli.com

To nerdy girls everywhere:
smart is beautiful!

—O—

# CONTENTS

# INTRODUCTION

I don't understand the difference between program management and engineering management so I don't see why we need this at Zendesk," said Morten Primdahl, cofounder and then CTO of Zendesk, during my second round of interviews for the role of creating a Program Management Office (PMO) for the product development organization. His comments were an auspicious start to say the least!

A year and a half later, Morten and I were walking along a street in Copenhagen, Denmark, where Zendesk was originally founded, having a very different conversation. "She's awesome!" exclaimed Morten, speaking about my (then) lead program manager for product development. When I pressed for details, he opened up:

> She's effective because she just blends into meetings, becoming part of the team. She's respectful about what's going on but keeps bringing up questions and picking up dropped balls in a very nonintrusive fashion. The team was struggling with how to move forward on developing a very

broad new set of services and she helped us break down the work into meaningful parts with a timeline that made sense. Her tone is always pleasant, and her demeanor just makes it a pleasure to work with her. In my past experience with project managers—the closest I've been to working with a program manager—that was just not the case. She's very much the exact kind of person I hope Zendesk can attract to help us keep things good while growing.

What a difference eighteen months can make.

Several months later, Morten visited the San Francisco headquarters of Zendesk. He stopped by to say hello and asked me how things were going, so I told him how the PMO had expanded and was continuing to grow. He marveled at the growth and the value the PMO brought to the company and encouraged me to write a book that would tell people how to do what I had done. Well, Morten, thanks for the encouragement! My goal with *Get on Track* is to offer information and guidance to companies and executives who are interested in creating a PMO, as well as individuals who are interested in becoming effective program managers or want to hone their best practices.

At its core, *program management* is all about strategic execution. A company has a vision for what it wants to become. That vision provides the foundation for a long-term strategy, and then a set of annual goals and desired outcomes to move that strategy forward. Program managers put in place programs to drive successfully to those outcomes ensuring that the work done by the teams they support is derived from those company goals (p. 11).

At its core, program management is all about strategic execution.

In contrast to *project management*, which is more vertically focused and more domain specific, program management is focused on broader strategic goals. Successful program management drives alignment between several organizations in one company—for example, engineering, product management, marketing, and sales—toward a common goal. That goal might be the release of a new software product or service, implementing support for the General Data Protection Regulation (GDPR), or rebranding the company.

When I started out in the industry, working in program management wasn't a career goal. I had no idea the discipline even existed when I was studying computer science in college. I've spent the majority of my career working in Silicon Valley with the exception of a three-year stint in France. Over my career, I've worked at small-, medium-, and large-sized companies and held roles in software development, product management, operations, technical support, and localization. Those experiences gave me a rich understanding of how software is designed, built, deployed, and supported and how companies of all sizes are run. It's worth noting here that although all my experience in program management is in the software industry, program managers are found in governments and across many industries, such as biotech and aeronautics. The skills required for a program manager in any industry are generally the same. What varies is their subject matter expertise.

I first became exposed to the role of program manager when I was working in France. At that point in my career, I had worked as a software engineer, product manager, and technical support engineer and also spoke both French and English. I was asked to take on the role of technical program manager that required me to guide the delivery of product features from initiation to launch, collaborating as needed across product areas, functions, and regions. It was a perfect blend of my skill sets. When you have a room full of people each with their own motivations and differing views about how to approach a problem, it's good to know what is motivating that product manager, or what the engineering lead is thinking, as I did. I also knew that smart people don't like to be told what to do; that influencing without authority is the way forward. I've seen firsthand the importance of bringing the localization lead into the conversation early because this can be painful for global customers if localization isn't considered until late in the software development process.

Working in France also gave me experience navigating cultural differences. Language barriers are challenging and even more so when they occur across thousands of miles and in several time zones. Working in a "remote" office in Paris, France, far from the Silicon Valley headquarters, I experienced the entitlement present in the "home office" and the subtle expectation that the remote office should be the one adjusting working hours to the Pacific time zone. I watched as Californian slang was thrown around with abandon, confusing the heck out of the non-native English speakers, and throwing me into the stressful (and sometimes humorous) role of interpreter as I also tried to pay attention to what was being said in the meeting!

All my career experience folded neatly into my new life as a program manager, but it's my deep belief that the most important abilities for this role are people skills. An exceptional program manager needs a solid understanding of the business together with strong planning and scheduling skills and the abilities to break down complex processes into meaningful sections, effectively communicate program status, and successfully mitigate issues and risks. But it's people skills that make all the difference in this role. As a program manager, you need to build relationships with your team members and stakeholders and be empathetic to the team's needs and concerns. But you must also remain objective throughout the lifecycle of a program by keeping its goal(s) in the forefront and leading the team to make the right decisions for the business. Over time, that objectivity builds trust, which comes in handy when you need to nudge people in the direction required for program success. And finally you have to be likable, because even with all the other practical skills in your tool belt, if you can't get along with everyone (and I mean everyone), you simply won't be successful at driving programs forward.

Since my time in France, I've held program management roles and honed my craft in a variety of software companies. I learned the value of taking a proactive approach by getting to know the team and the business, building relationships, learning what keeps them up at night so risks can be mitigated and programs stay on track, establishing trusted partnerships with stakeholders, all with the objective of moving the needle on company goals. Done well, the role of the program manager has a huge impact on a business and also results in great job satisfaction for the program manager. Now, imagine a whole team of these talented, like-minded individuals centralized in a services function, collaborating effectively and building bridges across the company to deftly move the company strategy forward. This type of organization can be transformative!

When I worked at Adobe, other program management teams often asked me what the secret to my success was. Why were the program managers on my team creating so much positive impact on the teams they supported? At Zendesk, people often said things to me like, "We couldn't have done this without program management," or, "My team literally wouldn't exist without your support." As people left Adobe and Zendesk for companies around Silicon Valley, they realized I had built something unique and came calling for advice. I've distilled all that advice into this book.

*Get on Track* is designed to take you step by step through the process of creating a Program Management Office (PMO). Parts One and Two are about building and running a PMO. Part Three is about program managers who make up the PMO and how they can level up their game so that the teams they support will make the same transition Morten did—from skeptic to enthusiastic supporter of program management. At the back of the book I've created a roadmap (p. 226) for you to explore as you build out your own PMO, but please feel free to refer to the topics most useful for your own situation.

In this rapidly growing field, it probably comes as no surprise that there are several books that provide information on the standards and principles of good program management. But what is missing is a book about how to create and nurture a PMO in companies currently operating without one. This book is for the business leaders I've spoken with over coffee in recent years who want to build a top-notch PMO, and for the program managers who want to know how to make program management work best in their company and what kind of people they'll need to make that dream a reality. It represents all the effort I've put into developing the best practices that I still use today. So, please consume it with gusto and feel free to contact me at paula@pauladieli.com if you would like to know more.

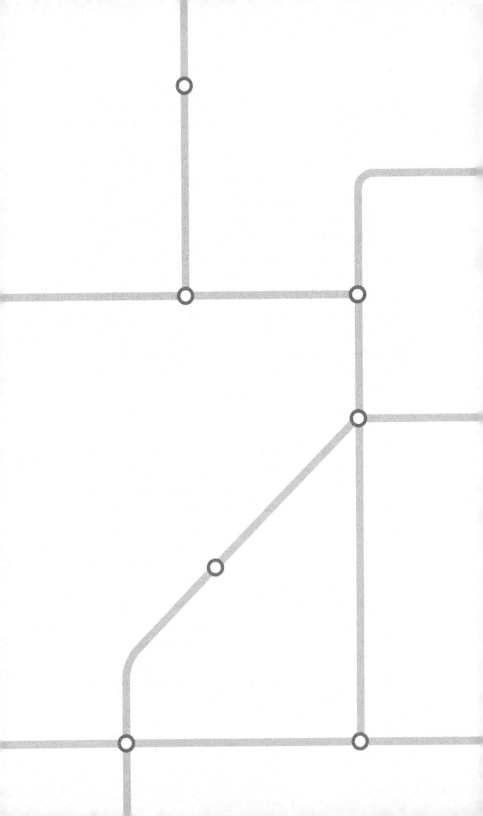

# PART ONE

# BUILDING YOUR PROGRAM MANAGEMENT OFFICE

# 1

# WHAT IS PROGRAM
# MANAGEMENT?

—o—

In the introduction, I referred to program management as strategic execution. The programs we put in place and drive forward are based on an understanding of the company vision, long-term strategy, and annual plan. But when I describe program management to businesspeople who might not be familiar with how it works within a company, I like to use a metaphor of a train to describe it—the sleek high-speed train (in French it's called the TGV or train à grande vitesse) that whisks you into Paris. And on that speedy train, program managers are the train conductors.

When you are a train conductor, you are bound to ask and answer a lot of questions. For example, if the train is going from San Francisco to New York, you might be asked by a passenger how soon you'll arrive at your destination and what stops the train will make along the journey. The conductor needs to know what the train's route is, what the schedule looks like, how many passengers and staff will be on board at each stop, and who is responsible for tickets, meals, and repairs, as well as what to do when things get snarled. You'll pass out passenger surveys at your train's final destination to measure the success of your service.

Similarly, when a businessperson tells me they need a program manager, there are things I need to know to help them arrive at their destination on track. I need to know where the business is trying to go and how quickly. How will this program move the needle on the overall company strategy? Have commitments been made already? Is there a plan in place and who is involved? And what's the driving factor behind the program? This could be something like releasing a product feature as quickly as possible or making sure the product meets the needs of the customer. Then we develop a plan that includes goals, timelines, resourcing, roles and responsibilities, and measures of success. I'll talk more about that planning process later in Chapter Four.

Once the train starts moving, communication is a monumental part of what program managers do. Passengers like and need to know what's happening along the way. In program management, formal communication takes place during cross-functional program team meetings (or program meetings for short): we align everyone on the next several milestones, make decisions to enable progress, communicate and discuss plans that have cross-functional ramifications (such as pricing or launch plans), and resolve any issues that may have cropped up. Status reporting is another type of formal communication in which we communicate program status, usually via email. But informal communication is equally, if not more, important than formal communication. When you drop by someone's desk, hang out near the team you support, have coffee with key program team members, or build relationships with stakeholders—these are the times when the program manager learns what's really going on.

Like a train conductor, a program manager is focused on cross-functional coordination. They bring in the various program team members at the right time. Some team members, such as those in engineering, might be along for the whole ride. But other teams, such as the legal department, may not need to get on the train until later, when marketing content needs their review. It's important that the program manager can count on each program team member to do their job, but they won't get into their business unless there's an issue. This is just like the train conductor who doesn't get involved in what the menu looks like but needs to know the food supplier will be at the station in the right place and at the right time.

Program managers need to be proactive. They need to know what the next few milestones (or train stops) are and to understand and mitigate risk. For instance, if the train is traveling through the Rocky Mountains in November when winter storms kick up, a good train conductor will call the track maintenance team ahead of time to ensure the branches overhanging the tracks are cut down before the train comes barreling through. They've taken this route before and know that if a branch or tree were to fall and block the tracks, it could slow down the train or, worse yet, bring it to a screeching halt. They know who their stakeholders are, who they can count on to deliver, and who or what has been problematic in the past. Similarly, if the program manager misses something that slows the program down or even halts it in its tracks, they'll address the issue to get it moving forward again. Good, proactive program managers are always mitigating risk. They're always thinking about what could go wrong and putting things in place to ensure they don't.

Train conductors need to balance the needs of the train's personnel and its passengers, especially if there is an issue like a delay or a missed stop. To do this effectively requires a cool head. Likewise, program managers must work objectively. The people working on a program often have diverse opinions, and it's the program managers who facilitate conversations without taking sides and drive everyone to the decision that ensures the program's goals are being met. Objectivity builds trust. When there is trust, program team members or stakeholders will alert the program manager to a risk (ideally before it becomes an issue), knowing that the program manager will solve it objectively in the best interests of the program.

Finally, a good train conductor is always checking in on the progress of the train's journey and making sure the goals for the trip will be met. Program managers typically use retrospectives at the end of a program but often also upon completion of key phases, or legs of the trip, so they can make improvements along the way. A well-executed program ensures that the business runs as effectively as possible and that passengers are likely to return.

Now that you know how program management works in a company setting, are you ready to get on board?

## What's the Difference between Program and Project Management?

Let's clear up something right away: there is a distinct and crucial difference between *program* and *project* management.

I'll talk more about the alliance and partnership between program and project managers in Chapter Six, but for now it's important to know the difference.

*Program* management drives the end-to-end design, development, and delivery of a program at a cross-functional level to achieve the broader strategic goals that support the company's vision. *Project* management is vertically focused and more domain specific: deep rather than broad. Project managers are in a specific domain or function, such as engineering or IT, and focused on leading a set of subject matter experts, such as software engineers, systems analysts, or network engineers.

*Program* management is the process of managing multiple related projects headed toward the same result. A program can be large or small, long-term or short-term, and is usually made up of several projects or workstreams. The program might be a new product launch, for example, but the projects or workstreams might include the engineering work, launch plan, security review, and pricing and packaging. Program managers therefore drive alignment between several organizations in a company—such as engineering, security and compliance, product management, marketing, and sales—to reach a common goal. And a group of *projects* is called—you guessed it—a *program*.

When more than one stakeholder is involved, things can get sticky. Strategic cross-functional or cross-company programs usually involve many different stakeholders with distinct agendas and diverse opinions. Unfortunately, the communication gap between organizations in a company (read: silos) is sometimes more like a chasm. Program managers are there to bridge those chasms.

## When Should You Add Program Management?

The simple answer to this question is when it's needed! But how do you recognize that your company needs program management?

When someone creates a software start-up, they hire software engineers first and then maybe a product manager or two, as well as the usual support staff needed for running a small company. Sometimes a recruiter or a top-notch administrative assistant may be added into that mix. Often program management isn't added into a company until it doesn't fit in one room (or small building), or perhaps when the company begins to expand across several geographies, often due to an acquisition. That's when communication between organizations in the company gets challenging and silos begin to form. Work that is specific to an organization and doesn't require outside help is what we call a project (in contrast to a program), and teams generally can and should handle that work themselves. But when the work requires more than one organization within the company, that's when things get complicated. Enter program management!

One of the secrets to the success of the PMO I built at Zendesk was that it filled a specific gap just like this. One of the most pressing issues when I joined Zendesk was cross-functional coordination. This gap between organizations is still the hurdle that companies find the most challenging. As our PMO had only two program managers at that time, it was critical that we focused on the most important cross-functional efforts to get them successfully across the line and in doing so demonstrate our value. I told Adrian McDermott, the president of product development and my manager at the time, that he could pick five cross-functional efforts for program management to work on, and as we completed those, we could take on more work. The reality is that each of the managers in the PMO could drive several large and a few small programs simultaneously. But we stayed focused on the top priorities to get some successes under our belt and prove the overall value of program management.

As the Zendesk PMO team grew and took on more programs, it was important to go where we were welcome. A few people resisted getting us involved and so we stayed away from those situations until they were sure about us and our impact. As Adrian would say, "Don't poke the bear!" To this day, my mantra remains the same: focus on the highest priority programs, and go where our participation is embraced.

## Ask Questions First

Once you decide to build a PMO within your company, it's time for socialization. I'll talk about this in more detail in Chapter Three, but it's a good idea to talk up the function of program management early in the game if you want it to be a success. Employees need to know what the PMO is, what the program managers will do, and how the PMO will help move the company's vision forward.

During the first program I drove at Zendesk, the PMO wasn't well known within the company. When I sat down with the newly assembled program team to understand their requirements, the executive sponsor stared at me and said, "Who are you, and why are you asking me all of these questions?!" Since then, I always socialize the PMO before starting with a new program team member to make sure they understand how program management works and how we will move the company goals forward.

When people are aware of your purpose and how you work, your kickoff meeting is likely to be more productive. Program managers usually start with the kinds of questions considered basic in information gathering or problem-solving: who, what, where, when, why, and how.

First, *why* do you need program management involved?

- Is the effort cross-functional?

- Is the business suffering from a lack of communication between functions?

- Is there a big group of projects that are all part of a broader goal that should be driven as one program?

The business owner or product owner, with the backing of the executive sponsor, should determine (or they should already know) the answer to this question. If not, then "Do not pass Go! Do not collect $200!" Ask the sponsor or business owner to figure out the why and get back to you before you continue. The *why* is foundational for all the other questions a program manager needs to ask.

Once you get the *why* settled, the *what* questions are next:

- What's the problem to be solved?

- What are the goals/objectives and how do they support the company strategy?

- What information exists already?

- What are the component parts to the program (multiple projects or workstreams)?

- What's the primary driver?

- What do we optimize for (scope, schedule, or resources)?

Next the program manager needs to know *who* will be involved:

- Is there an executive sponsor?

- Is there a business owner or product owner?

- Who are the key stakeholders?

- Who is already involved in the program? Who else needs to be involved?

- At what level are people involved? What are their roles and responsibilities?

Then *how* are we going to get this done?

- How will this program be resourced?

- What risks might impact the program?

- What are the dependencies?

- Are there competing priorities?

- How will we know if we are successful?

Next tackle the *where* questions:

- Where are the resources located?

- Where are the dependent teams located and how will that impact their ability to collaborate?

Finally the program manager will get to *when* this program will take place:

- Is there a schedule?

- Has anyone already committed any dates to management or customers?

- Are we making any scheduling assumptions?

You may not be able to get answers to these questions immediately, but the more information a program manager has about the program's needs and expectations, the better. One thing program managers are not afraid of is too much information!

Now that we've covered the basics around what program management is, when to bring it into a company, and when to begin the all-important socialization process, the next chapter will focus on how to build the PMO.

## Key Takeaways

- Program managers drive the design, development, and delivery of a program at the cross-functional level in service of the company vision.

- Add in program management when cross-functional coordination is a challenge and organizations aren't communicating well across functional boundaries.

- Focus on the top priority programs in the early stages of creating a PMO to demonstrate value and ensure success.

- Socialize the PMO within the company early on so that people understand what program managers do and how they can help move the company toward its goals.

# 2

# LAYING DOWN
# THE PMO TRACKS

—o—

Before you begin building your PMO, take a look at the roadmap at the back of this book (p. 226). It provides an overview of the steps you need to consider in the overall process. To get started, here are three important things to address initially before you can hire in earnest and begin driving programs forward:

1  Determine how to structure the PMO. Should it be centralized or not?

2  Figure out how the PMO headcount will be funded.

3  Make sure the company is diverse in its hiring procedures by collaborating with the human resources department and through team training.

## Should You Centralize Your PMO?

Program management is a services function and there are various considerations when determining whether to centralize:

- Company size
- Company structure
- Program manager effectiveness

When I began the PMO at Zendesk, I had the luxury of starting from scratch, which meant that I could set up the organization in the way I believed would be most effective and I could hire the right talent for the job. I was creating the PMO for one organization only, product development. I didn't give any thought to whether I was going to centralize the PMO, as it wasn't relevant at the time. Zendesk was still a fairly small company. That said, I learned early on that consistent program management processes, tooling, and communication mechanisms are important to stakeholders, especially as it became clear that program managers would be needed across the company and I was creating the program management function from the ground up.

Our initial programs were a new product launch and a rethinking of our pricing and packaging strategy. These programs were by their nature cross-functional. We worked with the usual suspects in product development: product managers, engineering managers, and software engineers. But in both these cases, we were also working with people from marketing, IT, and customer support.

After several months, the IT manager we were working with on the pricing and packaging program began to see the value of the cross-functional coordination we were providing and asked if we could help IT with some cross-functional work that could really use our expertise. My first question to him: Did he have any headcount to hire a program manager? No, he answered, but it was something he was thinking about. (If I had a dollar for every time I heard that . . . )

Channeling my manager at the time, Adrian McDermott, who always put company needs first, I shrugged and smiled and asked what he needed help with. He was interested in completing a migration of customers from one system to another to simplify things for them. The work was what the software industry calls tech debt, and a vestige of an acquisition that "we'd get to when we had time." Anyone heard that before? Yeah, I thought so. Well, it was going to require more than a year of work, and everyone said it couldn't be done. (Any program manager worth their salt takes that as a challenge!) When I brought the request to Adrian, he asked me what he always does, "What is the right thing for Zendesk?" Needless to say, we took on the work, which was driven by a senior program manager who wanted to prove the naysayers wrong (she's like that) and assisted by a dedicated engineering manager from product development who knew this important work required his partnership with IT. The work got done in about a year and a half, earning the engineering manager a (very good) bottle of whiskey. And then, lo and behold, the IT manager showed up at my desk with a headcount for a full-time IT program manager!

Around the same time, our VP of Creative came to me and said, "I have this person on my team who I think is doing the same thing you all do, and she's really good, but I don't know how to develop her. Could you take her into your group while

# Create comfort through consistent processes.

we still pay for her and she continues to support our team as program manager?" You bet. So this was how the centralized PMO came into being at Zendesk—organically. People saw the positive impact we were having, and they wanted more of it.

As the PMO hired a few more program managers and gained exposure across the company, people liked walking into a program meeting knowing how it would be run. They liked easily locating the weekly status reports in their inbox, all written in the same format, using the same green/yellow/red status measurements (p. 134). There's a certain comfort in consistent processes. It avoids redundancy, which was critical for the small yet fast-growing company Zendesk was at the time.

Few companies and program managers have the luxury to set things up initially the way they'd like. So what should you do if your program managers are not part of a centralized organization or if centralizing the PMO is not an option? One solution to this conundrum is to create a PMO council made up of PMO leads from across the company. I've seen this work at companies of various sizes. This happened during my time at Adobe and, at this writing, it still exists today. The council comes together informally on a periodic basis. They drive consistency around processes. They produce a program management newsletter to share best practices. And they organize annual PMO offsites for continuous development and team building. They can speak with one very effective and persuasive voice on issues which effect program managers, such as desired changes to the job ladder and job architecture. The council is led by a senior PMO leader for a six-month stint, at the end of which a PMO leader from a different business unit takes over. This does require a group of employees with the motivation to devote the time to the effort. This type of structure may not be quite as effective as a centralized PMO, but it sure adds value and perhaps makes more sense for a company of that size.

I've spoken to enough small and fast-growing companies that started out with a decentralized PMO. Functions independently started hiring program managers. Not surprisingly their work and approach evolved inconsistently. And the various functions aren't communicating; the program managers are just as siloed as everyone else. They realize a centralized PMO can be a solution to their problems. In that case, consider promoting a PMO leader from within the company or hiring a seasoned PMO leader to bring together the program managers from across the company to form a centralized team that efficiently and effectively drives cross-functional programs forward.

At a start-up or smaller company, centralizing the PMO function in the early years is a great way to ensure the function is set up in such a way that the role is well defined and the PMO runs well, which is important in a high-growth company. After the PMO becomes well established, and the company has grown enough that it's now divided into divisions or business units, it's not unusual for services organizations such as a PMO to be split up too. The program managers will already know each other well, and they'll be working in a consistent way. As long as they continue to communicate and share best practices, the goodness that was created in the early days will live on.

Centralized or not, program managers exist to streamline execution of programs and make things run better. And you can't argue with that!

## How Should You Fund Your PMO?

There are various options for funding a PMO and I strongly recommend you think about this carefully when building a PMO. I joined Zendesk to form a PMO for product development and that specific organization funded my role and the first ten or so program managers I hired. As we received requests from organizations outside of product development, each organization was asked to provide the headcount.

The benefit to this model is that the organization has skin in the game. It is active on the field of play, sharing in both the success of the program manager they are funding and the work being done by that program manager. The organization providing the headcount funding shares the responsibility. They determine the priorities for their organization, and the program manager drives forward those highest priority programs. Additionally, they don't have to worry about finding, training, managing, and developing their program managers as that is handled by the PMO.

For example, suppose the organization that wants a program manager is marketing, which is responsible for driving awareness of the company and its products. The marketing team engages, educates, and nurtures prospects, is responsible for the customer buying experience and for retaining and expanding the customer base. They want program managers to support their team, but their expertise is in hiring product marketing managers, communications managers, and digital marketing specialists. They want a high-functioning program manager, but they don't want to spend their time and expertise hiring, developing, and managing one. They prefer that the PMO makes sure the marketing team has a well-trained and happy program manager (or three).

The potential downside to this funding model is that the organization may decide to pull the funding if they don't see the value in the program manager's work, or if there is a higher priority need for that headcount elsewhere in their organization. That's certainly their prerogative. I consider the PMO to be a service organization that serves at the pleasure of the head of the organization that funds one or more program managers. That's why it's important that the program manager meet and exceed the needs of the organization they support. Then the organization won't want to use the headcount for anything but the wonderfully productive program manager!

Other options might include funding the PMO from a general budget. This model works well for program managers supporting general and administrative (G&A) organizations where it's harder to identify which organization has the most at stake for a program. For example, many G&A programs involve IT, finance, and legal organizations, all of which are contributing at the same level to the effort. The downside to this funding model is that each organization won't have a say in how much PMO support it gets. Also, the PMO will be dependent on funding from a part of the company that often doesn't have a healthy budget. Case in point: if the main business of the company is building software, product development usually has a larger budget than G&A. A hybrid approach can work here, where all functions except G&A fund their program managers, and the G&A organizations use a general budget.

The plus side to a general fund for program managers (assuming you get enough headcount) is that the PMO can decide which programs are assigned program managers and how much time they spend on each. This allows for the flexibility to move program managers around as business needs change.

The most important thing is to put in place a funding model that works for your company, which supports the way the various organizations within the company are structured and funded.

## Building Diversity into Your PMO

Diversity and inclusion are tremendously important issues when you are staffing the program management office. For example, a 2018 *Forbes* article written by Bonnie Marcus called "What Does It Take to Keep Women in Tech Companies?" shows that more diverse companies are more profitable and create more long-term value. To that end, when building out a new team, I highly recommend ensuring the team is diverse when it comes to ability, age, ethnicity, gender, race, religion, sexual orientation, and socio-economic status/class. Diversity leads to innovation, inclusiveness, creativity, better decision-making, productivity, and higher profits. Diversity and inclusion are critical if you want to avoid having a team of program managers who approach problems in the same way.

A funny thing happened on the way to creating the Program Management Office at Zendesk. There were two program managers already on staff, one man and one woman, so we were split evenly from a gender perspective. Most of the people I hired next happened to be women. Also, since I was initially hired to create a PMO for product development, the background of these people tended to be in the software development industry.

As time went on, I started to get comments from my peers about the lack of gender diversity on my team. I bristled at the feedback. I mean, I spent ten years as a software engineer and out of all of the teams I worked on, only once was I *not* the only woman! And at the time of these comments, I was the only woman on the product development leadership team.

Okay, so I had a bit of an ax to grind, but I accepted the feedback nonetheless, as it was valid, and I believe that lack of diversity of any kind should be addressed. My next step was to enroll the team in interview training because that's where sensitivity to diversity has a big impact. We received guidance from our People Operations team on general interviewing techniques, the importance of diversity, types of diversity, and how to ensure the interview process would lead to diversity in hiring.

Freshly aligned on the importance of diversity on our team, the team agreed to focus on improving gender diversity as that was the primary focus of the company's Diversity and Inclusion team at the time. Since then, the company has expanded its diversity goals to hire more candidates who are Black, Indigenous, or people of color, which may also lead to better gender diversity numbers.

During this process, I also flagged the fact that we seemed to be ruling out candidates who didn't have a background in software development. There were a few raised eyebrows around the table at this statement, but I encouraged the team to be more open-minded. A team of program managers with the same background is problematic for obvious reasons—they all think the same way and may miss unique solutions because they're all coming at the problems with the same biases.

The program manager job description was then rewritten by a program manager with a background in recruiting. Here's how it read: "We've found that a bachelor's degree and ten-plus years' relevant work experience in a global technology company across a global organization are the most common predictors for a successful program manager at Zendesk... We expect you to... You have a demonstrated ability to... " Sound familiar? But here's the kicker. The job description also invites all to apply with this inclusive statement: "That said, if your experience looks a little different from what we've identified and you think you can rock the role, we'd love to learn more about you."

As we reviewed résumés for a program manager to support our technical operations team, we found a great candidate with a background in—wait for it—the transport industry. She didn't know what the agile methodology was and had never program managed in software development, but she had all of the most important skills needed for the role (p. 170). Her most recent role had required her to program manage a team of transportation professionals who had to rip up and replace a set of train tracks in a forty-eight-hour period before the train came barreling through. I figured that if she could do that, she could handle a team of engineers responsible for deploying cloud-based software, and I was right. She was a quick study: she swiftly learned the technical topics required for the role and flourished in it.

As a result of those inclusive interviewing practices, Zendesk now boasts a team of program managers with backgrounds in tech, healthcare, criminal justice, food advocacy, recruiting, security, marketing, and organizational behavior, among others. They're brilliant, supportive, and collaborative.

They help each other out with best practices, tips, and strategies for success, and the company values the contributions of each program manager and celebrates their individuality. Diversity and inclusion go hand in hand when it comes to optimizing your talent. Inclusion means ensuring that everyone has a seat at the table. That everyone feels comfortable sharing their opinion, particularly if it diverges from the direction of the conversation. Leadership can reinforce this by encouraging everyone, especially the quieter voices, to speak up and by challenging the team to come up with ideas outside the prevailing opinion. Ensuring psychological safety means that everyone in the room feels comfortable participating and sharing even when they have a different opinion, idea, or approach. After all, there's no point in hiring diverse candidates and then not getting the most out of them!

## Key Takeaways

- Structure the PMO to ensure maximum operational efficiency, which is so important in the early stages of a company's growth.

- Centralizing a PMO has advantages such as streamlining procedures and avoiding redundancy.

- Explore the various ways to fund the PMO, such as a model where the organization requesting a program manager funds the headcount but leaves the management of the program manager to the PMO. This can be combined with a centralized funding model to meet the needs of all types of organizations.

- Train the PMO on the importance of diversity and inclusion, build it into the hiring process, and ensure the work environment is inclusive.

# 3

# BRANDING THE PMO

In the early days of the PMO at Zendesk, some colleagues had the impression that a program manager would do "whatever needs to be done." Others tried to tell me what they thought program managers should be doing and clearly had no understanding of the role. Rather than saying that, of course, my response was, "How about we sit down, and I can walk you through what we do in the PMO."

When I first created the Zendesk PMO, Adrian McDermott wisely suggested that I develop a slide deck about the PMO and undertake a tour of the development centers around the world—there were five at the time. Adrian knew there would be questions and consternation about what we were creating. I spent some time creating a deck that covered why the PMO exists, the team's one-liner, what program managers do, how they do it, and how to engage with them, along with a high-level organization chart.

Over the next months, I visited those five offices to present the deck at an all hands or lunch and learn. After my presentation, there was usually a lively Q&A session with strong, constructive questions and feedback. During those visits, I also met with key business leaders to learn more about them, their roles, and their teams. In one meeting, the engineering manager, who had previously worked at a large computer company, was worried that the creation of a PMO meant Zendesk was going all "big company" on him. He thought I was going to put a project manager on every scrum team and make them do Gantt charts. At the time, I had two program managers and there were twenty-plus scrum teams. So no, I told him, that wasn't going to happen (not to mention that program managers normally only use Gantt charts for more complicated programs).

As the months went by, I continued to deliver that presentation to anyone who asked about the PMO. Sometimes I would do so informally because someone had made a snide offhand remark such as "Why do we even need this? What does a program manager do, anyway?" I would hear the remark first- or secondhand and gently offer to set up a meeting with the people asking the question so I could walk them through the deck. I also realized the value in reaching out to new leaders even if I was first met with "Oh, I know what program management is. I worked with program managers at ABC Company." In those cases, I politely replied that we do things a bit differently (read: more effectively), then I would proceed with the meeting. Afterward, they would remark that we did seem to be doing things a bit differently (read: better) and would thank me for reaching out. Often they would reciprocate, telling me about their team as well. As Humphrey Bogart said in *Casablanca*, this was "the beginning of a beautiful friendship"!

I also delivered the deck as the first session in the Zendesk program management onboarding. It was my way of communicating our philosophy to new program managers, and speaker notes were included so that anyone in the PMO could deliver the presentation to their peers, teams, and stakeholders. One outcome of this is that other organizational teams at Zendesk have been inspired to create their own "branding" presentation to help socialize their team's purpose at the company. Yes, imitation is truly the sincerest form of flattery.

I can't stress how fundamental it is that everyone at the company understands what program management is and what to expect when engaging with the program managers. Socialization lays the groundwork for ensuring program managers are invited to the right conversations and meetings where strategizing and planning takes place. Those conversations and meetings give program managers the context for why a specific program is important, explain the team's goals, and reveal how the program will move the company forward.

It's important to note here that helper personalities are especially attracted to the role of program manager. That sometimes results in a program manager who wants to be a jack of all trades, which can make it challenging for others to understand their true purpose. I am careful to brand the purpose of program management—that it drives the end-to-end design, development, and delivery of a program at a cross-functional level. I also make sure program managers are doing the work they're supposed to be doing and not getting distracted by tasks that take them away from the things only program managers can do.

Program management is such an overloaded term, so these talk sessions (however they take place—quickly or more

# Invest energy in crafting your PMO brand.

formally) are invaluable in clarifying what it is program managers do and how they work. Once your PMO is ready to go, your team should be able to give a short five-minute version of what the PMO does or a longer forty-five-minute explanation as appropriate. That's why you need to spend some time crafting your brand.

## How to Brand the PMO

When I created my brand presentation, I had no idea that I would still be delivering a version of it several years later. It's probably one of the most useful things I did as I built the Zendesk PMO. So what should you include in a branding presentation? Here are four main sections I recommend.

### 1. Tell them who you are

The first section of your deck should talk about where the PMO sits in the company. If it's a centralized organization, note that it is a services organization and show a dotted-line reporting structure to all of the members of the leadership team. At Zendesk, most of the program managers are funded by each organization (p. 29) and all reside within the centralized PMO. At Adobe, the PMO is decentralized and program managers report into their functional organizations. These are the two most common organizational structures. Some companies have a hybrid approach, where some larger teams have a centralized PMO and others have program managers reporting into the teams they support. However your PMO is organized, it's important to describe that, and an organization chart is usually the best way to do this.

## 2. Explain what you do

The bulk of your presentation should be focused on what program managers do. Start by describing the difference between program and project management, since that's a common question (p. 14). Then I use the train conductor metaphor to describe what program managers do (p. 11).

**If a program is a train, then the
program managers are the train conductors**

Align with cross-functional stakeholders on **where** to go

**Plan** the best route to reach the final destination
with minimal roadblocks

Ensure people know **roles and responsibilities**
and foster **communication**

**Drive** the train and **proactively** assess the landscape
to anticipate issues and risks

**Mitigate issues and risks** to keep the train
moving forward **on track** and **on time**

The next thing to include is a slide with key verbs that describe a program manager's day-to-day work. I used the figure below at Zendesk and it effectively drove the point home about the valuable work a program manager does.

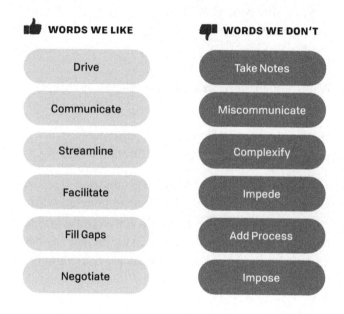

| 👍 WORDS WE LIKE | 👎 WORDS WE DON'T |
|---|---|
| Drive | Take Notes |
| Communicate | Miscommunicate |
| Streamline | Complexify |
| Facilitate | Impede |
| Fill Gaps | Add Process |
| Negotiate | Impose |

Then the presentation should talk about strategic execution and how program management translates company strategy into a set of portfolios and/or programs to realize company goals. As a way to concretize all of this information, I like to include examples of recent programs from a variety of organizations such as marketing, product development, IT, and sales. This helps people understand the wide variety of work performed by program managers.

**3. Demonstrate how people can engage with the PMO**

It's important to ensure those in the organization you support understand how to engage with the PMO. Here are the five main points I include:

1   Describe the work that takes place in a program's early stages to drive alignment across the cross-functional team.

2   Explain how the PMO is resourced.

3   Walk through the process for how program managers execute a program.

4   Discuss the important process of gathering feedback during and after a program's successful completion.

5   Talk about how the program manager partners objectively and closely with the business lead to understand their requirements and program goals. A successful program requires a tight partnership between the program manager and the business lead as their roles are complementary (p. 109). See Table 3.1.

TABLE 3.1

| | Planning | Execution | Wrap-up and Retrospective |
|---|---|---|---|
| **Program Manager** | Facilitator | Program driver | Close, conclude, and learn |
| **Business Lead** | Visionary and approver | Active participant and decision maker | Outcome owner |

#### 4. Here to help

Finally, I walk through some more detailed organization charts so it's clear who will be working with whom, and then close with a reminder that program management is there to help them (their organization), their teams, and the whole company to work better to successfully achieve the company vision. After all, that's what the PMO is all about!

## What's in a (Program Manager's) Name?

In the context of program management, the name matters: the judicious use of the program manager title is critical because indiscriminate use can create confusion with stakeholders.

Program management is a discipline in and of itself, just like product management, product marketing, or software development. Program managers exists at many companies and they perform a particular role, as specified by industry standard job-leveling structures such as Radford's global job-leveling framework. No matter the organization, program managers all work in a similar way and are developed and measured using job descriptions based on those job codes.

Initially the Zendesk PMO had just one experienced program manager besides me. Interestingly, there was a Program Management Council in existence with about a dozen members. My manager asked me to figure out what those folks were doing. I hoped they might be a source of experienced program managers that I could bring into the PMO. Instead I discovered that this council was made up of people from several teams such as communications, marketing, and executive administration. None of them were actual program managers but all of them had wanted a different title that made them sound more important or professional, and they had decided "program manager" was it.

Although I empathize with people who want more respect for the good work they are doing, I was introducing a PMO into the company for the first time. I defined a methodology, created a job ladder and associated job architecture, began socializing the concept of program management across the company, and was driving cross-functional programs forward. The role of program manager had to be clearly defined alongside the specific things we do. If the title was used for many different roles, that was not going to help.

After I began facilitating the council and continued to socialize the PMO, it quickly became clear to the council members that what they were doing and what I was doing were quite different and the group petered out naturally. Problem solved. At a company like Adobe, everyone knows what program managers do, so socialization of the role isn't required. But at a less established company, it's important to continuously socialize the work program managers do until it's crystal clear that most people understand the role. This means meeting with the executives, leaders, and subject matter experts on a program team and taking them through your branding deck to explain the role. As people join the company, you'll need to socialize the PMO with them as well.

In many industries, program manager is a title that is still misused, even though industry experts and respected organizations such as the Program Management Institute (PMI) define the role in a specific way. This is probably because program managers are a newer role to people than, say, a product or project manager. So your communication efforts will be worthwhile. In your deck, you might also take the opportunity to define similar sounding roles such as project manager or product manager so the differences are clear.

If you're creating a centralized PMO from scratch, I recommend you work with your People Operations department to ensure that organizations outside the PMO don't create roles or recruit people with the program manager title. Insist that the only people allowed to use the title of program manager belong to the centralized PMO. This will be hugely important as you build out your PMO.

As a company grows, and people constantly rotate in and out, some folks may still use the title improperly. You'll hear about them by way of your stakeholders and partners around the company who get confused when someone with the program manager title does something different from normal. This mishandling of the role name introduces confusion, which you'll likely hear about. Just reach out to the offender and politely explain that the title is reserved for members of the centralized PMO. Offer to partner with them to find a more appropriate title. Most people will understand and comply.

Program management is a discipline practiced by professionals who are highly skilled and well trained in the discipline that is strategic execution—objectively driving complex cross-functional programs forward in order to execute on the company strategy. I'm proud of the work program managers do and the critical role we play. If your PMO is new, continue to socialize that work and protect the title until it's unnecessary. Oh happy day!

## The Value of Learning the Business

As you socialize and brand the PMO within the company, you have a terrific opportunity to get to know more about the business and organizations you will support, and that's important for your success.

I began my program management career in product development, and it's where I have the most experience. But I've managed programs for teams in G&A, sales, marketing, and even did a stint driving a program for creative. I'm enriched by my understanding of many parts of our business, and as a result, I can more effectively lead and support my team of talented program managers. A solid business understanding is also crucial when you are working to get an invite to strategy sessions, something I'll talk about in the next section.

Every program manager needs a good understanding of the business from the perspective of the organization they support. For example, if you're an engineering program manager at a software company, you understand how software is built, what the development lifecycle looks like, how testing is done, and how solutions are deployed. You have enough technical background to understand how the work and the teams are structured and what the usual challenges are (such as performance, scalability, and reliability).

Does this mean a program manager must have a background as a software engineer? No, definitely not. Would it help? Sure, to a point. If you speak the same language as a software engineer, you'll be able to converse freely and understand technical conversations more readily. There's also less of a chance you'll have the wool pulled over your eyes (not that an engineer ever tries to do this!).

So what's the downside? A program manager needs to consider what's best for the program rather than be swayed by the opinions of team members, particularly those with whom they have a strong working relationship. If a program manager knows a lot (read: too much) about software development, sometimes they find themselves intrigued by one solution over another. They might forget to focus on what's right for the program when distracted by an elegant technical solution, even if it's not the most appropriate from a time-to-market perspective. At this point, the program manager has lost objectivity—and I speak from personal experience!

A similar thing happens when a program manager lacks experience in a certain organizational function; they'll need to quickly learn about the business as they begin working with that team. When I worked for the creative organization in Zendesk, an organization I had no prior experience in, I didn't have a foundation of knowledge to lean on. But I studied hard to learn about the work being done in product design and branding, and I learned things I'd never thought about before: why the creative organization is so important to a company and how their work manifests in products, marketing messaging, recruiting, and company culture. This focus on learning the business certainly made me a more effective program manager for that particular organization.

Even today when I step in for program managers who are temporarily absent, I find this is a good opportunity to learn about the businesses they support. First, I study on my own, reading whatever materials are available about the business and the work in flight. Often I then ask the business leads to walk me through their priorities and goals. I ask what the executive in charge of the organization is worried about and what their business leads are excited about. This is a great way to get up to speed enough to advise on next steps, or to help unblock a team and move a program forward.

Learning about other businesses around you is also a good idea since the job is cross-functional coordination; it's likely that, at some point down the road, that knowledge will come in handy. To that end, I recommend all program managers moonlight on other teams whenever possible and when appropriate. At Zendesk, one of the G&A program managers wanted some variety in her day-to-day work, so she ran a program for the social impact team (p. 190). She learned about how that team functions and contributed to the great work that it does for the community where the company's headquarters is located. It was a win-win situation for all involved.

Program managers need to understand the business enough to have sufficient context to effectively do their job and understand what they are program managing. Here are three steps toward achieving that.

## 1. Ask questions

Find out how the work in the core business gets done. If you are in the software industry, ask to see the software development life cycle (SDLC). Ask the technical folks to explain how the product is built, what technologies are being used, what the product roadmap looks like, and what processes and methodologies are in use. If the organization is on the go-to-market side of the business, ask how the teams are set up, what roles exist, how they interact, how they price and sell the product or service, and how they ensure customer success.

## 2. Take all training offered to employees

Whether this is product, sales, or technical training, program managers should take any training offered. This is an excellent way to grow a program manager's knowledge about the business. To this end, business leads should consider offering the program manager whatever training the business puts their employees through.

## 3. Initiate whiteboard conversations

These conversations are helpful for elaborating everything from an organizational structure to an inbound marketing campaign to a software architecture. Once there's a basic understanding of how things are set up and run, program managers should ask where the challenges and pitfalls are, what the risk areas are, and what keeps the business lead or executive sponsor of the program up at night.

Once a program manager has clarity on the business, they can more effectively run a meeting to keep everyone aligned on the business objective(s). They know how important a particular issue is, as they will have already elaborated the program risks into a risk register and can more effectively mitigate those risks. They'll be better able to pinpoint resource gaps as they know what work is in progress and what's left to be done. With a solid understanding of the business, program managers are simply that much more effective.

## Getting Invited to the Party

Socializing the PMO and learning about the business is all well and good, but if the program manager isn't then invited to the table, they won't get the opportunity to show business leaders how program management can be an essential part of achieving goals. It only works well if you are brought into the game early on.

Too often a team spends a few days, weeks, or even months working through a problem and discussing potential solutions. They go offsite to dig in on what they should and can accomplish, what the road ahead looks like, what the risks are, how they will staff the work. And then they return to the office set up and rarin' to go. Suddenly they realize they need a program manager to drive the work forward and that's when they reach out to the PMO.

Okay, so let me get this straight. You spent several days discussing all the things that a strategic program manager needs to know to effectively drive forward a complex program, and only now you want to bring one in? If you read through the program meeting kickoff questions that I talk about in Chapter One (p. 18), you'll know that an opportunity has been missed by not including the program manager in those early conversations. Now they will have to ask questions about the things the team already spent several days discussing without them.

When this happens to me, I gently chide the requestor for not including the program manager in early discussions, and often they respond with "But you don't want to hear all of that, do you?" Yes, I do! Program managers want to be a part of all those discussions. They want to be privy to the wrangling that got you to a decision about whether, when, and how to move forward. They may sit quietly and take it all in, but they do want a seat at the table. Trust me—you want that program manager in your meeting!

It is crucial that program managers participate in strategic level planning meetings. Ideally, they should be brought in *prior* to kicking off a program. These strategic discussions often take place at a team offsite, at an organization's leadership meeting, during the annual planning cycle, when teams are preparing for a management review, over lunch or coffee... you get the idea. The goal is to have the program manager present when teams are discussing future strategies and release roadmaps so that they have the same context as the rest of the team that they will be supporting.

Managing a program is not done in a vacuum but in the broader context of the work of the team, their organization, and the company. If a program manager comes in with a cursory understanding of the bigger picture, more than likely they'll work less effectively without all of the information they need to start strong. But how many times has a program manager been asked to manage a program about which they know nothing? This happens more than you'd think, and more than I'd like. So, program managers, how do you make sure you get that invite? The first step is to learn about the business, the charter, and the goals for the organization you support, as discussed in the previous section (p. 48).

When you are meeting with business leaders and other potential partners, ensure you are actively listening and ask follow-up questions or for clarification. I love learning about new technologies, and my favorite way to do this is to ask a team member to draw me a picture of their existing product or solution and what they are building; you might consider that technique if you're a visual person. As you ask questions, listen and learn. You'll get more interested and hopefully excited about the subject at hand, and this is a key part of building a relationship with that team member. As you wrap up these conversations, ask for an invite to the appropriate meetings.

For the program managers out there who get the invite, make the most of the opportunity. Don't sit quietly and simply listen (you won't anyway). Ask for clarification, surface dependencies (also known as "connecting the dots"), point out risks, and ask the questions that others neglect to ask. Better to ask now rather than later. Definitely don't offer to take notes (p. 138). If asked (that can happen when people don't understand your role), suggest someone else in the organization take them as they have more context (or you conveniently have carpal tunnel syndrome). Instead, focus on asking questions that enable you to join the conversation:

- What do you foresee as the biggest challenges to implementing that idea?

- How are you thinking you'll measure success for that initiative?

- This sounds like a pretty large initiative. Have you thought about breaking it down into phases?

Connecting the dots is another useful technique, and one that program managers are eminently qualified to do. Here are a couple of suggestions to make along these lines:

- You might think about talking with So-and-so who tried a similar thing / is doing something similar / will want to hear what you're doing.

- Have you considered that there may be dependencies on such-and-such teams?

If these techniques fail to get you included in the meeting or invited back, if it's appropriate, offer to be the objective facilitator for the meeting and then do a bang-up job. This requires you to work with the business leads up-front to determine goals for the meeting, decide on an agenda, and clarify attendees. And then you'll be armed to effectively facilitate the meeting by ensuring the right topics are covered, everyone is participating, and goals are met. And while you're there, be sure to ask questions and actively participate. You're a program manager, so you can multitask with the best. Bear in mind that it's during this process that a program manager builds relationships with the people they'll be working closely with over the next few months, maybe even years. Eventually someone will walk up to you during a coffee break and say how glad they are that they thought to include the PMO.

## Developing a Taxonomy

It's important early on in the journey of building out a PMO to develop a taxonomy, where you should name, describe, and classify the work program management does. For example, what do you mean exactly when you use the terms project, program, or portfolio? It makes it easier to communicate with the teams you are supporting if you clarify the work the PMO is doing. With a taxonomy in hand, you can align the program management team and the external team members and stakeholders with consistent terms.

I recommend you create your taxonomy by learning about taxonomies that already exist in your company. Whatever product it is that the company makes, find the architects or senior people who make it and ask to see what they are using as a taxonomy. In a software company, this person is usually the software architect (in a biotech company, it might be the research department), and the taxonomy will be centered on a software development lifecycle. Included in the taxonomy will be things like requirements, design patterns, architectures, methods, defects, and tooling. Once you've reviewed whatever taxonomies are available, you can determine what your PMO taxonomy should include, and you can clarify where there are overlapping concepts or redundant terms.

For a PMO taxonomy, simply speaking, there are big programs, medium-sized ones, and small ones. The large programs are usually made up of one or more portfolios, each aligned to a business goal or requirement. Within the portfolios, there are several programs, and perhaps a smaller portfolio that also contains programs. If people are inconsistently using terms to describe something complex, you can see how quickly and easily things can get confusing.

As discussed earlier, the terms *program* and *project* are often used interchangeably (p. 14). The slide deck I use to introduce the PMO to new hires describes the difference between a program manager and a project manager. The deck is a high-level introduction (p. 41) and doesn't go into more detail than that, but a document that describes your taxonomy will contain more specifics. Here's what to include:

- Define the taxonomy and each item (portfolio, program, etc.) within it.

- Define and illustrate the relationship between each item.

- Establish a RACI (responsible, accountable, consulted, informed) matrix so responsibilities are clear. For example, a *program* manager drives a program forward but a *project* manager or business subject matter expert is responsible for project success.

- List the operational considerations that describe how these items are executed daily. For example, if a project, program, or portfolio has processes associated with it, then you should note that the program manager will engage the operations team to define and/or refine it.

- Create a comparison chart as a useful reference for understanding the taxonomy. See Table 3.2 as an example but use what makes sense for your business.

A great way to solidify the reader's understanding is to take a couple of typical programs and draw the taxonomy in the context of those programs. Include portfolios, programs, projects, and the relationships to each other. Then describe the roles and responsibilities of the key players, including a sample RACI for a large program or portfolio. See Table 3.3 for an example of this.

**TABLE 3.2**

| | Project | Program | Large Program | Very Large Program |
|---|---|---|---|---|
| **Definitions (PMI)** | A temporary endeavor undertaken to create a unique project service or result. | A group of related projects managed in a coordinated way to obtain benefits and control not available from managing them individually. Programs may contain elements of work outside of the scope of the discrete projects in the program. | | |
| **Program Manager** | No | Yes | Yes | Yes |
| **Program Meeting** | No | Yes | Yes | Yes |
| **Executive Sponsor** | No | Yes | Yes | Yes |
| **Steering Committee** | No | No | Yes | Yes |
| **Status Reporting** | ... | ... | ... | ... |
| **Business Value** | ... | ... | ... | ... |
| **Benefits & Deliverables** | ... | ... | ... | ... |
| **Timescale** | ... | ... | ... | ... |
| **Scope** | ... | ... | ... | ... |
| **Resourcing** | ... | ... | ... | ... |

| Portfolio |
| --- |
| A collection of projects and/or programs and other work that are grouped together to facilitate effective management of that work to meet strategic business objectives. |
| Yes (Multiple) |
| Yes |
| Yes |
| Yes |
| ... |
| ... |
| ... |
| ... |
| ... |
| ... |

TABLE 3.3

| Definition of / Change to | Executive Sponsor | Steering Committee | Program / Portfolio Team | Delivery Team |
|---|---|---|---|---|
| Vision and Strategy | R/A | C | I | I |
| Scope | A | C | R | I |
| Schedule | R | C | A | I |
| Resources | A | R | C | C |
| Design | ... | ... | ... | ... |
| Architecture | ... | ... | ... | ... |
| Pricing and Packaging | ... | ... | ... | ... |
| Marketing | ... | ... | ... | ... |

Once your taxonomy is in place, share it with others in your PMO. Gather their input and incorporate any required changes. Then share it with other teams who have their own taxonomies to ensure you're in alignment. Consider sharing the taxonomy at a high level at the start of a program to confirm all are clear on the language that will be used throughout the program to describe the work and who will be doing it. Finally, always walk through the taxonomy when onboarding new program managers, in order to ensure your own team is using the right terminology from the get-go. This will avoid confusion and misunderstanding, especially in the middle of a complex program when clarity is key and time is of the essence.

## Key Takeaways

- Branding what program managers do is critical, and socializing should start early in the game. Tell everyone about your team and the role.

- Create a presentation that effectively communicates the PMO brand. Talk about what you *don't* do as well as what you *do* so that expectations are set correctly.

- Assign all PMO leaders and individual contributors the task of socializing the brand.

- Limit the use of the program manager title to people in the PMO or who are doing that role (in a company where the PMO is decentralized) to protect the brand thereby ensuring a clear understanding of the role.

- Program managers can more effectively drive programs for the organization(s) they support when they have a solid understanding of the business.

- Business leaders should invite program managers to the table whenever strategic discussions take place.

- With a clearly defined and communicated taxonomy, your program management team and your external team members and stakeholders will use a common language around programs and program management.

# 4

# ALL ABOARD
# FOR SUCCESS

—◯—

Once your nascent PMO is created, you'll need to consider setting up and running programs and doing it effectively to achieve program success—the crux of the program manager's job. Done well, a program should have a powerful impact and be rewarding for the team, the program manager, and, of course, the company. Let's dig in.

## Setting Success Measures for a Program

When I worked at Macromedia, the programs I drove centered on a software development kit (SDK) that we licensed to companies that used it to create a graphical user interface for their products. So rather than creating success measures around the end customer who was several layers beyond our work, our success was measured simply by delivering said SDK to the partner company. But sometimes the success measures for a program aren't as straightforward.

The first program I drove at Zendesk was a complex one that involved most organizations at the company and about a quarter of the company's employees. As I worked to understand the business objectives for the program, I naturally asked the business lead, a product manager, how we would know if the program was successful. What I received in response was an annoyed look that I had seen before and then the brush-off: "I know what you're asking is important, but we can figure that out later." Uh oh, I thought. This one's going to take some patience.

Fast-forward a few weeks and we were in a program meeting (p. 12) walking through the detailed timeline to ensure all participants understood what was expected of them. Since a cross-functional program meeting is the usual forum for discussing and agreeing on program success measures, the program manager can ask the business lead to come to the meeting prepared with a proposal so that the team has something to react to. In this program, there were some tricky interdependencies that required the collaboration of everyone, along with a lot of complex work. That same business lead/product manager was impressed at what was involved and, realizing the wisdom of setting success measures up-front, suggested that we figure out how we could be sure all the work would be worth the effort. "What a great idea!" I said. "Let's do that."

One of the critical tasks of the program manager is to ensure that teams measure the right things. Success measures are how you know if you've met the strategic/business objectives for a program and could be evaluated by customer usage, customer migration, customer conversion, revenue, or customer churn, for example. Often several smaller projects are part of the program, and the success of those will likely ladder up to a broader program objective. Ideally, success measures are clear and simple. SMART (specific, measurable, achievable, relevant, time-bound) goals, OKRs (objectives and key results), or a simple goal focused on process, performance, or outcome will work. Some companies tend to operate more effectively with fewer goals because they're easier to remember and focus on. Whatever the goal-setting criteria, it's best to use what the company culture prefers.

Sometimes, teams choose success measures that don't connect to the business objective. For example, success is defined as shipping a product or releasing a feature. These outcomes are certainly positive steps along the way to achieving a business objective, but they don't tell you if the customer likes the feature or if the rate of customer adoption will lead to expected revenue goals. I would argue that knowing you've actually solved a problem for the customer is the true measure of success.

I remember a bright product manager who looked at the usage data her engineering team had built into the software. A few weeks post release of a new feature, she was astonished to find that not one single customer was using it even though she heard many customers ask for it. This was a real head-scratcher, but usage data doesn't lie. The product manager reached out to a few customers who had requested the feature and was surprised to learn that they had been unable to locate it. She regrouped the team and they redesigned the user interface (UI) so that the feature was more prominent. They tested it with the customer, and voilà, they were now able to find it, use it, and report back to her that they were happy. If she had not reviewed the usage data, she and the engineering team would have continued on, believing their work was finished!

# Measure the right things.

The program manager has an opportunity early on in the program cycle (but even later if required) to influence the team to set the right success measures. Success may mean different things to the various functional team members, so the savvy program manager may need to level up the conversation to the strategic goals, to what the business is expecting after your program is complete, which may be weeks or months after you think you're done. In that case, the program manager is responsible for getting the band back together to review the results and determine if more work—say a tweak, or even a phase two of the program—is required to solve any residual issues. If, as described above, you have an intelligent business lead who follows up to validate the results, all the better!

## Measuring the Impact of Program Management

When it comes to setting goals that evaluate their own impact, program managers often struggle to come up with something measurable. They might say things like, "We can't really measure our impact because while we are responsible for program success, no one reports to us, so we have no direct control over the success or failure of a program." Nonsense. You can *absolutely* measure your impact. Here are three ways to do this.

### 1. Positive feedback

One way to measure your impact is through positive feedback. The people you support may say things like "She's awesome!" or "Things just run better" or "I don't know how we'd get anything done without him!" Although this feedback is great to hear, it is of limited value. What you need to know is what makes them say this. So, first say thank you, and then ask what it is exactly about what the program manager is doing that makes them respond so positively. Usually you'll hear more useful things like, "She has a unique way of letting us all voice our opinions but then getting us to align on a decision so we can move forward." Or, "I know that if I share a problem we're facing, he'll be all over it and will quickly move the team toward a viable solution." Now this is the kind of feedback you can work with and use to encourage the specific behavior that's resulting in program success for that team. Something else to consider is surveying for feedback. In the early days of the Zendesk PMO, we periodically sent out a survey that measured the Net Promoter Score (NPS) of the teams we were supporting. If program management was scoring an eight or above out of ten and teams were happier than before we arrived on scene, then we were doing something right. The measurement goal can look like this:

*Exceed Net Promoter Score (NPS) of 8.0*

## 2. Effective risk mitigation

Program managers spend a good part of their efforts on risk mitigation, which has a direct impact on whether or not a program succeeds. Risks that are starting to increase should be mitigated quickly by the program manager such that the program never has a red (blocked) status. When they see smoke, they jump on it so quickly that it never becomes a fire. This is possible if risks are thought through at the start and throughout the life of a program. Then when a risk is increasing, the program manager quickly identifies the appropriate mitigation plan and begins tamping out that smoke. This behavior definitely has a positive impact on the program, and that activity can be tracked and measured. The associated measurement can look like this:

*In 90 percent of high-impact, high-likelihood risks for the program there was a documented mitigation plan underway within a week of the risk increasing.*

Even with the best laid plans and continuous and effective risk mitigation, program managers must be prepared for change. The train may have slowed or even stopped (in other words, a risk is now an issue) and the job of the train conductor (program manager) is to get it moving again at full speed. What to do? Jump all over that issue and close it down! Promptly gather the right people together and determine how to solve the problem. That effort can be measured like this:

*All high priority issues for the program were resolved within two weeks of occurring.*

If a program manager's schedule slips, does that mean that they're not doing a good job? Well, if they've done a great job mitigating risk and quickly closing down issues, that gets the program most of the way there. If the reason the program schedule has slipped is due to an unforeseen competitive strike or a worldwide pandemic (for example), then it is harder to make that case. In the case of a competitive strike, the product manager should be encouraged to stay on top of industry competitors, but secrets are often closely guarded, which means this may still happen. The jury on the pandemic is still out!

### 3. Efficient communication

A third example of how to measure a program manager's impact is less specific from a measurement perspective but is still a valid goal to shoot for. A big part of a program manager's job is continuous communication with stakeholders to ensure their needs are being met by the program. Happy stakeholders will tell you that their program manager stays in regular contact to update them on changes so there are no surprises during the lifecycle of the program. Measuring that is as simple as the PMO manager asking all of the key stakeholders if they feel their program manager is effective at meeting their needs. The goal might look like this:

*When surveyed, 100 percent of stakeholders said the needs for their programs were being met by their program manager.*

Strategic execution is a critical function that program managers perform within a company, and it can and should be measured. These suggestions for measuring the positive impact you have as a program manager will go a long way to assessing your effectiveness.

## The Importance of Scheduling

Imagine you are driving a train from San Francisco to New York. There are no other stops. All you know is that you must arrive in New York seven days after departure from San Francisco. If a passenger who needs to arrive in New York on time for an important meeting asks how we're progressing, you can only shrug your shoulders and say that you don't know because you have no way to track progress to the destination without intermittent scheduled stops. That passenger will probably feel anxious about having no way of letting their boss in New York know whether they'll arrive on time. Now, imagine this scenario as a program without a timeline. What would the response of your team be if your status report says, "I think we're on schedule but I'm not sure"? Yeah, that won't go over well.

When a program manager sets up a program, they work closely with the team to define a plan from start to finish that meets the business objectives. That often means they are in the unenviable position of asking for milestones and dates. Sometimes scheduling is the hardest task for a program manager when setting up a program because the team might be reluctant to provide dates. They may not yet know enough to provide dates they can stand behind. Or they're wary of committing and then not being able to follow through. It's also not easy to estimate work that has vague requirements, especially if you're at a high-growth company whose work is innovative. Arriving at milestones and dates for brand-new work can be challenging. The work needs to be broken down into the smallest chunks possible, at least down to weeks and often down to days. This is much easier to approximate when the discovery and design phases are complete, but the reality is that estimates often need to be provided well beforehand.

A program manager should start this crucial conversation with an explanation of why a schedule is important for the program manager, the key stakeholders, and management, which is so they can plan ahead and make commitments to customers and shareholders. They may encounter resistance when pushing teams to provide that level of detail and commit to it, but it has to be done. I had one engineering manager say with exasperation, "Why are you so focused on dates?" It isn't about the dates—it's about having the ability to tell if the program is on track. The program manager is on the hook to provide weekly status to key stakeholders and management; to do that, they need a level of comfort about whether the team is on track. They can't do this without a timeline for the work.

Now if that same engineering manager provides me with their best estimates based on known information, past experience on similar efforts, plus advice from key team members, my ability to track progress is much improved. At least I have an idea of what's expected, can explain to management that the schedule is tentative, and then adjust the schedule and related status as needed, keeping everyone in the loop at all times. It's not perfect, but it's better than nothing and it's often the reality of developing software!

Another objection I often hear is that if a team provides dates and then they change, the team will look bad. Well, that's what change management is for. I explain that task C took slightly longer than expected and why that is, and then adjust the schedule. For example, it's not ideal if I tell you three days in advance that you need to reschedule your meeting in New York, or to let the head of sales know a week before a planned ship date that the feature will be delivered three months later. But if a program manager has as much notice as possible so that they can communicate changes to the stakeholders, it is definitely workable. With enough notice, people can adjust their plans. They won't love it, but they'll understand. As engineering VP Bill Finch from Hewlett-Packard used to say to me, "I don't like being disappointed, but I really hate being surprised!"

How can a program manager navigate these tricky waters to get the timeline they need to effectively manage the program? As mentioned earlier, start the conversation with an explanation of why a schedule is important for the program manager, the key stakeholders, and executive management. Everyone needs to know how the program is progressing and if it's on track. Enough time should be given to the team to create a schedule they can stand behind, even if it's not exact. The program manager can negotiate with management for some give and take as needed. The engineering manager should understand that the program manager has their back and will mitigate continually to ensure the team has the best shot at meeting their milestones. As long as the team is communicating regularly and transparently with the program manager, they can in turn let stakeholders know if there is risk so they can adjust their plans as needed and well in advance. And if a date slips despite best efforts, the program manager will ensure the information is reported accurately and fairly.

A program manager can also help the reluctant manager arrive at a draft schedule by asking how long each task will take: a day, a week, or a month. A month? Oh no, it won't take that long! A few days? It's more complicated than that—two weeks is a good estimate. Now we're getting somewhere! This approach is painstaking, but after a couple of practice rounds usually the manager will go away and work on a schedule and come back to the program manager with something they can use as a foundation. If trust is already established between program team members and the program manager, this process goes faster with far less angst. And if the program manager does a good job at managing up during the program, there is less finger pointing and more understanding when changes happen—and they will. As with most things a program manager does, good clear communication is what it's all about!

## How to Create a Program Schedule

Consider the schedule something that the program manager carries around in their (virtual) pocket at all times. It's their train timetable, if you will, and they're constantly reviewing it to determine if the program is on track. A program has clear start and end dates, and the schedule is used to guide the program manager through its lifecycle. The main stages of a program schedule usually are:

- Discovery
- Implementation
- Validation
- Launch
- Retrospective

Each of the above stages includes a set of cross-functional milestones that might look something like Table 4.1.

Depending on the complexity of the program, sometimes a Gantt chart may be preferable to a table. Note that this program schedule will likely link to several more detailed functional project schedules, in the above example for engineering, localization, and documentation. The program schedule only includes cross-functional milestones and is generally less detailed than each functional project schedule.

The program schedule is kept up to date by the program manager on an ongoing basis and is usually updated before the status report is written (p. 78). The updates are gathered continuously as the program manager meets with the various stakeholders throughout the work week.

**TABLE 4.1**

| Status | Date | Milestone | Description | Owner | Notes |
|---|---|---|---|---|---|
| On Track | May 2, 2021 | Imple-mentation begins | Coding of the feature set begins | Jamal | Includes phase 1 features only |
| On Track | May 16, 2021 | Docu-mentation begins | Online help | Jennifer | |
| At Risk | Jun 10, 2021 | Localiza-tion begins | Localization into 20 languages | Yoko | Resource constraints |
| At Risk | July 15, 2021 | Implemen-tation ends | Coding of the feature set is complete | Jamal | Includes internation-alization work |
| Not Yet | Aug 1, 2021 | Retrospec-tive held | Team retrospective for all geos | Bianca | Will be held remotely |

Any items that are at risk or delayed/blocked should be discussed with the owner, and any issues that require cross-functional team members should be discussed at the weekly program meeting. The types of issues surfaced will be related to changes in scope, schedule, or resources, in other words those that can't be resolved with just one or two program team members. The business lead, executive sponsor, and stakeholders should be alerted by the program manager when there is any hint of a change in the schedule that will cause a delay.

## Kicking Off a Program

You are ready to get the train moving! But before the journey begins, everyone should know when they're getting on and off and what to bring when they board. Some people may board the train halfway through the journey, and it's the program manager's responsibility to make sure they know their stop.

Once the program schedule is in place, the program manager should gather together the team members from each function for a kickoff meeting, which will be the first in a series of weekly cross-functional program team meetings. (I'll talk more about them below and again in more detail in Chapter Seven.) In that kickoff meeting, you will review the program goals and schedule, discuss any open issues, and make sure everything is in place to get to the first couple of milestones. That meeting agenda will look something like this:

- Welcome
- Program goals
- Success measures
- Review of schedule
- Roles and responsibilities
- Q&A

The business lead will present the program goals and success measures since they're the subject matter expert and the one setting the program requirements. The program manager will go through the schedule and roles and responsibilities, and then any questions should be addressed. By the time this kickoff meeting is over, everyone should leave the meeting inspired and excited about the journey ahead. Now you are ready to board!

## The Program Team Meeting

Once you've kicked off a program, you'll gather together most of the same people who attended the kickoff to a program team meeting on a regular basis. I call this a working meeting since it's the forum used by the cross-functional program team members to do the following:

- Review progress and plan what's required to keep moving forward on a timely basis.

- Review risks that may be increasing and what is being done to mitigate them.

- Review issues that may have surfaced and proposed solutions. Decisions will be made here so that progress continues.

- Remind the team what needs to be done to reach the next couple of milestones on schedule and assign future agenda items accordingly.

The program manager prepares the agenda and sends it out to the attendees ahead of the meeting. The agenda is in a shared file the attendees can access to suggest topics for discussion and alignment. Example topics include clarification of program goals, review of and alignment on requirements and plans, and discussion of issues and risks. Dependencies should be reviewed to check that the team has what they need from others outside of the program team. Note that these topics require the active participation of the attendees, so the program manager should ensure the right people will be in the room. If a team member can't attend, they should send an appropriate replacement so that their absence doesn't negatively impact program progress.

The frequency of the meeting will vary based on where you are in the program timeline. For example, the program team may initially meet on a biweekly basis. As the team moves from discovery to implementation, they may decide to meet more frequently, usually weekly. After program completion, the team may sync up monthly to review progress toward program outcomes. See more on running effective program team meetings on page 123.

It's the program manager's responsibility to ensure a well-run and productive meeting. This periodic sync is critical to program success!

## Effective Status Reporting

Like train conductors who announce upcoming stations, all program managers in a company should have a consistent way of status reporting to make it easy for stakeholders know what to expect. This key task is a good opportunity for program managers to stop at the end of each week and reflect on where things are and pivot as needed. Think about what needs to be communicated and which risks or issues should be the focus of the next week. Bottom line, status reporting is the best way of communicating program updates at regular intervals to program stakeholders.

Depending on your company's preferences, you may use a variety of different ways to log status reports. In the past I've used Confluence; for complex programs, a custom Smartsheet template. Usually status reports consist of upcoming milestones, changes to plan (scope, schedule, or resources), issues, risks, program manager name (in case a stakeholder has additional questions), and the status color—typically green, yellow, or red (p. 134). Status reports should include a link to the program documentation such as a web page or plan so that if readers have more detailed questions, they can find the answers easily. When reports include status on several programs, it's a good idea to include an executive summary at the top of the report. This allows for a quick perusal and then a click down into the details as needed.

The biggest value of status reporting is that it allows a program manager to step back at the end of the week (or two weeks or month for programs that don't change very often) to evaluate how things are progressing. This is the time to zoom out from the details you might be focused on (say a missed milestone or a particular issue you're dealing with) and do the following things:

1   Review any changes to the plan: in scope (such as a competitive threat that warrants a course correction), schedule (something is taking longer than planned), or resources (a team member has been reassigned).

2   Determine what changes need to be discussed with program team members and communicated to stakeholders and management, as appropriate, prior to sending out the status. Have those conversations to give people a heads-up.

3   Update your program documentation accordingly, based on any changes, so that when the reader links to this documentation from the status report, the information is consistent.

4 Update the risk register and consider which risk(s) you should focus on in the following week, or what mitigation strategy may be more effective.

Reassessing program status may mean a quick physical or virtual walk around to see your program team members and chat about how things are going to catch any changes to plan or any new issues or risks. A program manager needs to remain objective during this process so that their report isn't influenced by a team member who may complain that the status is not green. The status report is the program manager's objective view of how the program is progressing and must be fair and accurate to give the stakeholders an unbiased view. A yellow or red status isn't bad; it's simply a reflection of the innovative nature of the work being done and the dynamic context in which the company is operating. Yellow or red should always be accompanied by an explanation as to what's being done to get the program back to green.

As a program management leader, I use status reports not only as a way to understand the status of the many programs the PMO has going at one time, but also to determine if the program manager is on top of things. If I click from the status report to the more detailed plan and it's not up to date, or the risk register appears light or empty, I'll start asking questions. If I see typos in the report, that reveals a lack of attention to detail, and I'll dig for more information. Although some program managers think I obsess a bit about status reports, they are a reflection of how effectively the program is being managed. And that's something about which I really do obsess!

## Key Takeaways

- Clarify how you will measure the success of the program to ensure the team's hard work won't be for nothing.

- Measure the impact of program managers as well. Even though their work requires soft skills (p. 170) that may be harder to measure, they play a pivotal role in program success.

- Schedules are vital. You wouldn't start a train trip without knowing where you're going and how long it's going to take. Because programs are strategic and cross-functional, make sure you have a good schedule in place and that everyone is aware of and aligned with the key milestones.

- A program kickoff allows everyone to understand the program goals, get on board with the schedule, and confirm who's doing what. It also builds momentum and team spirit to carry you through those rough patches.

- Status reporting is critical to keep stakeholders apprised of program progress. It also helps the program manager take stock of progress and focus on the right issues and risks.

# 5

# ISSUES
# AND RISKS

Good program managers know that where there's smoke, there's fire. They hold fire prevention classes and make sure everyone has a functioning extinguisher on hand. They wake the team out of their stupor and alert them when something doesn't seem right. If team members are smart, they listen to the program manager. Risk and issue management are different yet related exercises, and if one is done extremely well, the other one can be, well, mitigated.

## How to Manage Issues and Risks

As part of onboarding a new program manager, I like to include a session on risk and issue management. Although there is overlap between these two topics, it's super important to understand the difference. When I am describing the difference between a risk and an issue to a new program manager or a stakeholder, I like to keep it simple. A *risk* is an uncertain event that would have a negative impact on the program if it occurs. Risks should be mitigated by a program manager so that they don't occur. If a risk does occur, it is now an *issue* to be dealt with and closed in order to get the program back on track. Mitigating risks and closing issues are two pivotal activities for program managers. Risks should be thought about in the early stages of a program, in the context of what you could call a pre-mortem. The program manager involves the team in an exercise where they imagine the program has failed. Then they work backward to determine what could lead to that program failing, and how to keep that from happening. This is an effective way to get the team to own some of the responsibility throughout the life of the program for a positive result.

If risk mitigation is tackled early on, there are usually fewer issues to deal with during the lifecycle of a program. But risk mitigation involves a lot of advance planning and imagining the worst that can happen. Program managers who are on the ball think about these risks in a clear-eyed way, on an ongoing basis, and work proactively to keep the train moving smoothly forward on the right track. Here are three tasks that a good program manager should be on top of to achieve this.

## 1. Classify risks early

When a program manager puts a plan in place for a program, such as the development of a new feature for a software solution, they've worked with their business leads and cross-functional program team members to develop and align on a plan that gets the work done in a timely manner. Part of the planning process includes creating a risk register—a list of risks that could potentially hamper progress. A program manager classifies these risks into those that are least and most

# Think about risks in the early stages of a program.

likely to occur, and whether they would have low, medium, or high impact. Examples of common risks include scope creep, dependency on a shared resource, or poor communication causing confusion or lack of clarity.

Program managers do many things as part of their daily job and one of those is mitigating risk. They start with the things most likely to occur that carry the highest impact. They constantly work to mitigate those risks until the program is successfully completed. They ask what they, their team members, and any dependent teams might do to keep these risks from occurring. And when they smell smoke, they are all over it! Stamp out that smoke before it becomes a fire because if you are unable to do that, now you have an issue.

### 2. Resolve issues quickly

Once a risk becomes an issue, a program manager should be all over it until it's dealt with. Drop less important work, mobilize resources, quickly determine proposed fixes, and drive the team to a solution in a timely manner. Escalate the issue to the management level only if needed.

Some program managers list issues and risks together in a program page or status report. What bothers me about this is that one should prevent the other and how you treat them is very different, so my preference is to list them separately. Ideally, if you're obsessively focused on risk mitigation, issues should rarely occur. Some issues will occur that are hard to predict (COVID-19 is a good example), but most can be prevented with effective risk mitigation that's based on your past experience as well as that of your program management colleagues, program team members, or your manager.

### 3. Inform stakeholders continually

Program managers should involve stakeholders in the creation of the risk register so that their interests are represented. They should inform the stakeholders continually (usually via written updates) of the status of potential risks and how they would impact them and their team(s). If a risk increases, the stakeholder should expect the program manager to alert them of a potential issue so that they can adjust their plans as needed and possibly provide support. If a stakeholder doesn't hear from the program manager, they should reach out, especially if they see something worrisome in the status report. But this approach is only a backup plan as program managers should be proactive when it comes to keeping their stakeholders informed and involving them as needed in a mitigation.

## A Program without Risks Does Not Exist

One of my favorite activities on a Sunday afternoon was to read through the many status reports my Zendesk program managers sent out on a weekly basis. Okay, fine. I need a life! Seriously though, doing this as a PMO leader provides a good overall understanding of how the team is driving company strategy forward. I spend less time on the status of programs that are flagged green and on track, dig into those that are yellow, and definitely read up on programs that are glowing red.

Each status report includes hyperlinks to each program's more comprehensive page. If a program catches my eye, either because I want to learn more about it or to determine why things are going off track, I click into the program page.

I look at who the key players are, familiarize myself with the problem statement and how the team plans to address it—in other words, why this program exists. I scan the program timeline and make sure it's up to date (the sign of a program manager who's on top of things) and I scroll down to the risk register to see what risks the program manager is mitigating. Where is the program manager seeing smoke and what are they doing to stamp it out?

A good way to ruin my Sunday is for a status report to have an empty risk register. "How is that possible?" you might ask. Well, that's a good question. Every program has risks because there's always a chance that something will adversely impact its scope, schedule, or resources. Perhaps a competitor introduces a new product, an important task takes longer than planned, or a key resource has a family emergency... and the list goes on. A good program manager should have a handle on the list of things that could possibly go wrong and have thought through the likelihood and impact of each occurrence. These risks should be noted and reviewed by the program manager on a weekly basis, for example, when they're writing the status report. What's the one risk they want to surface on that report that is currently most relevant? And what's being done to mitigate it?

If a risk register is empty, the program manager probably hasn't spent time thinking through the risks, and it's unlikely they're doing any risk mitigation, or they're not mitigating the right thing(s). If a risk register is out of date or light on detail, you should question whether the program manager has a good handle on things. This might be a sign that they're overwhelmed with work and not prioritizing the most important work.

Good program managers spend time thinking about what could possibly go wrong and how to prevent it. This isn't because they are all doom and gloom, but because they live in the real world where the only constant is change. That means they need to be looking a few milestones ahead on their program timeline and determining what needs to happen to get the team there without delay. At its heart, this is what risk mitigation is all about. Every program has risks, but the savvy program manager is always mitigating them until the program is successfully completed.

## Are You in the Loop?

A junior program manager once shared a story with me about how their program/train went off track, a fire started, and they put it out and got the program back on track. They felt like a hero and asked me, "Do I get a gold star now?" Nope! Definitely not. Program managers get a gold star at the end of a smooth-running program, one where I never had to hear about a red status. If a program manager never *needs* to put out a fire, then they're a hero. And they do this by identifying their program's risks early in its lifecycle and then mitigating the heck out of them!

It's critical that program managers know what's going on at all times so they can proactively mitigate risks before they become issues. Good program managers already know when things have started to go south because they have established healthy relationships with their team members and are informed about any deviation to the plan. They make themselves available by getting around the office (either physically or virtually) so they're around when bad things are starting to happen. They drop by someone's desk or post a quick hello in a direct message or a chatroom app like Slack. Program managers often sit on the couches near the teams they support, and someone will usually drop by with some helpful information. A friendly "How's it going?" from the program manager might be met with a hesitant response, at which point the clever program manager will make room on the couch or offer to take that person to a nearby coffee shop where they may feel more comfortable sharing. I can hear my mother saying, "Mind your own business!" But in this case, their business *is* my business! (Sorry, Mom!) If I learn about a problem when it's too late, the schedule will have already slipped, and I won't be able to help the team recoup the lost time.

Besides the all-important informal information gathering that goes on, the rest of what a program manager learns about program status comes from a regular cadence of cross-functional program team meetings, where the team is reviewing requirements, marketing messaging, end-to-end testing, and strategy proposals. If an issue has surfaced, the program team members show up prepared to discuss the issue at hand and work as a team to brainstorm ideas, put proposals on the table, and work toward a solution. It's a good place for people to put their heads together, figure out plan B, and get the program back on track.

Colleagues at Zendesk often marveled at how program managers seem to know everything. They'd cruise by the program manager's desk to deliver some breaking news, and when the program manager didn't seem surprised, the refrain was usually, "But you knew that already, didn't you?" Yep!

## Managing Teams Across Multiple Geographies

A program that involves teams from around the world holds an inherent risk. I once observed an engineering team made up of US and EMEA employees work at cross-purposes because of lack of alignment on the architecture, which wasn't surfaced until well into the development cycle. This resulted in several months of delay and bad feelings that lingered even after the software was released. This kind of misalignment, along with a lack of communication, can develop quickly when people located in different buildings or geographies must work collaboratively.

Miscommunication and misalignment pop up even when everyone has been informed and is working from the same schedule, so the savvy program manager must always be watching for this. When it occurs, program managers play a pivotal role in gathering together teams that span multiple geographies. This involves meeting with program team members at all hours of the day and night to clarify program requirements, reconfirm stakeholder expectations, review and or revise the program plan, or continue to build relationships— yes, often across thousands of miles. Here are some tips for ensuring your multi-geo programs go as smoothly as possible.

### Understand the requirements

Traveling to meet in person is still the best way for a program manager to understand remote team members' requirements and to ensure these are in line with stakeholder expectations. If that's not possible, then an introductory video-conference meeting with key program team members will get this process started. You'll need several follow-ups with various team members and stakeholders to review what's been communicated, documented, and understood. Periodic check-ins between the program manager, business lead, remote team members and key stakeholder(s) are par for the course to keep things on track. This is usually done via the weekly program meetings, but other meetings should be added as needed. Another couple of smaller half-hour meetings over several months is absolutely worth the team's time.

## Build relationships

Healthy relationships with your team members and stakeholders are critical to a well-run program. Spending time on these relationships means less risk to the program and this relationship building is, of course, most easily accomplished when you're in the same office with the people you would like to get to know. But these days it's so often not the case, and there are several ways to establish these critical relationships regardless of location. One way is through a 1:1 meeting, and I'm a fan of having the program manager go to the other person rather than making them come to you. The PMO is a services organization, and you going to them sends a message that you're there to help them. If a program manager is meeting with a C-level executive, the expectation is that the program manager goes to the executive's office. If you are meeting with a peer, relationship building may be best accomplished outside the office over coffee. If the person in question is across the world, and it's someone with whom you'll be working for a while, meeting them in person, ideally toward the beginning of the program, is best, but should circumstances prevent this, a video call is the next best thing.

From there, regular check-ins across the miles are critical to program success.

These relationship building meetings can be formal, with a prepared agenda, or you can make them more informal, suggesting the other person bring their beverage of choice to the meeting or video call. This is a nice way to add some informality across the miles. And whether in person or remote, starting your meeting with something personal—such as asking the person about their weekend or how their home renovations are going—is a friendly way to ease into the conversation. It helps you build that all-important connection with that person.

## Don't skip the program kickoff

Whenever possible, you should get program team members and key stakeholders in the same "room" for a program kickoff to do the following:

- Clarify program goals
- Align on success measures
- Review roles and responsibilities
- Inspire and motivate the team

This kickoff is when relationships begin to be established and the various functional representatives begin to feel like part of a team. If it's not possible for all of you to be in the same physical place, the kickoff can be done with some people remote. Note that if several geographic regions are involved, this needs to be taken into account. For example, if AMER, EMEA, and APAC are all involved, consider holding two of the same kickoff, say one for AMER and EMEA, and one for

AMER and APAC, to keep one geo from having to get up super early or stay up super late. The kickoff will be followed by frequent (usually weekly) program meetings with most of the same people who attended the kickoff. Making this meeting effective is described in Chapter Seven, but it's important to note that the alignment problem outlined at the start of this section can be avoided if the program manager covers key decisions such as design, architecture, pricing, and launch details at the kickoff.

## Run effective virtual meetings

Well before the COVID-19 pandemic of 2020, program managers were already facilitating program meetings with people in the room with them as well as people across the world. Whether they use BlueJeans, Zoom, or Google Meet, program managers across industries know how to run an effective virtual meeting. As mentioned above, repeating the same meeting, or alternating between geos, say, every other week, is an effective way to keep in touch with team members worldwide without making people adapt their personal life to long work hours too often.

## Encourage team building outside of meetings

Adding a Slack channel for ongoing communication throughout the day is a great complement to meetings as it means questions get answered more quickly as team members in one time zone can ask questions that get answered as they sleep. And team building happens all day every day as people drop in and out as desired.

## Gather the team together

If teams are struggling to make progress across geos, it might be time to consider busting the budget and getting everyone together in one geographic location, even just for a week (p. 160). If this isn't possible, consider a long virtual meeting with people in the same virtual room for a few hours. Just leaving the line open, so to speak, while people are working away facilitates conversation. I've seen a team located in San Francisco get online once a week at six a.m. to allow for several hours of crossover time with their EMEA colleagues. Use your imagination! The important thing is that time together, whatever that looks like, promotes conversation and results in effective problem-solving that might save hours, days, or even weeks when all is said and done.

## Run a virtual summit

For long-running programs, consider a virtual summit held at, for example, the midpoint of the program, where the executive sponsor or business lead reminds everyone of the program goals, and the various teams demo their work in progress. This can be fun and motivating and may surface any areas where teams are misaligned. Breakout meetings can be used at a summit to dig into complex subjects or resolve ongoing issues. Video conference applications make this seamless. Then everyone can get back together for a motivating closing speech from the executive sponsor to remind everyone how the work they're doing will benefit customers.

## The Remote Life

In the Silicon Valley and elsewhere around the world, and particularly in the wake of the pandemic of 2020, the motivation to allow and even encourage employees to work remotely has increased. Meetings often happen over video with people working from home. Today's business leaders are wise to embrace this change rather than looking at remote employees as a hindrance or a deal breaker!

Although remote employees can provide significant benefits for business growth and productivity, the challenge is in building relationships between people who work together but rarely or never meet face-to-face. Since collaborating with remote workers is part of any program manager's job, I want to share with you some of my best practices for building relationships remotely.

- Meet face-to-face at least once if possible. It makes all the difference.

- Get your good mood on! Since your time together is limited, make the most of it. No one looks forward to meeting with a gloomy person who spends most of the meeting complaining or venting.

- Be present. There's nothing worse than distractions such as devices, the doorbell, pets (the other person may love seeing them, but barking in the background is annoying), or waving goodbye to your partner. All of these may signal to the person you are meeting with that they are not as important. Although these behaviors became more common during the pandemic of 2020, as the program manager you should do your utmost to make the person you're meeting with feel they're the most important person "in the room."

- Remember we are all human. Sometimes we forget the personal side of our colleagues. Whether you are sending flowers or a note of thanks, or simply saying thanks in a virtual meeting, when you genuinely acknowledge moments of job success, or ask about a sick child, the gesture is as much if not more appreciated by a remote team member than an in-person one.

## Key Takeaways

- Every program has risks and they will change throughout the program. It's critical that program managers know what's going on at all times so they can proactively mitigate risks before they become issues.

- The program manager should be laser focused on mitigating risks. If a risk becomes an issue, work with your program team to resolve it quickly to avoid schedule delays.

- Program managers play a pivotal role in bringing together program teams that span multiple geographies. Use the suggested tips and techniques and a growing number of video conferencing and messaging tools to facilitate global communication and effective remote working environments.

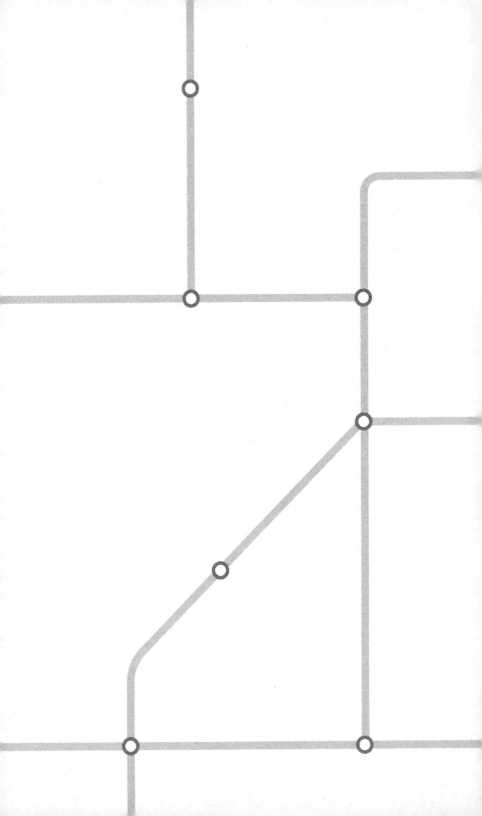

# PART TWO

# RUNNING YOUR PROGRAM MANAGEMENT OFFICE

# 6

—○—

# GET TO KNOW
# YOUR CREW

This chapter focuses on the team members who share the responsibility for keeping your program on track. Relationship building with business leads, executive sponsors, stakeholders, and project managers is vital, so I'd like to highlight how each role plays into the success of a program.

## Clarify Roles and Responsibilities

Zendesk was new to program management when I first started the PMO in product development. The company was still fairly small and was operating as a start-up in many ways. As I set up a program management framework, I was careful to explain how program managers did our jobs, so that teams wouldn't worry that we were going to encroach on their territory and get into their business. Most employees didn't understand that our role was about helping them achieve their broader goals.

For the first program that we drove forward, everything we did was new to the program team members. After holding several cross-functional program meetings, the talented senior program manager suggested it was time to review roles and responsibilities so that everyone knew who was doing what and what was expected from them. Since this exercise was new to the program team members, we decided to use a very simple RACI or a responsibility assignment matrix (p. 57) that looked something like this:

**TABLE 6.1**

| Responsible | Approver | Consulted | Informed |
|---|---|---|---|
| Ben, Jake, or Steven | Sam or Amanda | The program team members | The PM and dev teams |

When I look back on it now, I cringe at the lack of specificity in the RACI, but the PMO and the very idea of program management was brand-new to the company, and this basic version met our goal of introducing the topic without scaring anyone. I recall feeling nervous as the program manager displayed the RACI on the screen and walked the program team through it. I also remember that the team members were riveted. No, really! We didn't spend a ton of time going through it, but everyone got the gist. They thought it was super helpful and provided clarity, they got on board with their roles, and the program was delivered on time, even though it was wedged in between two immovable deadlines.

At the time, our executive sponsors, Sam and Amanda, known affectionately as Samanda, assured us that we could come to either one of them for key decisions and the other would fall in line. This guaranteed that a team member couldn't go to one sponsor, not like the answer, and then go to the other to see if they could get an answer they liked better—something that could have resulted in undesirable antics and confusion. Samanda held to their word and on several occasions when a decision was time sensitive, we saved time because we could go to whoever was available to get a quick decision.

As the PMO at Zendesk grew in size and sophistication, we used a variety of RACI matrices. RACIs can be fairly simple, or more complex where the program manager always outlines the specific decisions each person will be expected to make. I recommend you use the most appropriate RACI matrix for your program and make sure it's clearly communicated early on in the program lifecycle, ideally at the kickoff. With everyone aligned, you won't lose valuable time later figuring out who is responsible for a particular decision and then hunting them down to see if they agree. This way you can avoid adding risk to the program, have key decisions made on time, and keep to the timeline.

## Developing Effective Stakeholder Relationships

A good relationship with a stakeholder makes all the difference. I worked on a program at Adobe where the sales organization was counting on the delivery of a feature by a particular date so they could make a splash at the annual sales conference. I had kept the head of sales in the loop with weekly updates, either in person or via text message. I shared

# Not all stakeholders are equal.

the periodic ups and downs such that he knew if there was an issue, he would hear about it first. When an engineering issue meant a likely delay in the release of the feature, I wasn't looking forward to breaking the news to him, but I immediately let him know and he took the news calmly, thanked me for the early heads-up, and had plenty of time to find a replacement announcement that still managed to excite the crowd. It was evident that the time and effort put into that relationship was definitely worth it.

The stakeholder is a person or group of people who have a stake in the program outcome. As in the example above, if you are driving a program to release a key new feature of a software product, the stakeholders are the sales team who relies on that timely release so they can sell the product to new customers, as well as the end customers who will use the new feature. If you are introducing a new human resources information system to the company, your stakeholders will be the internal employees who will use it for recruiting, performance management, learning and development, and more.

Developing effective stakeholder relationships is one of the most important things that program managers do. I recommend these four simple steps to set up a program for success:

1   Get to know the people counting on the success of the program to achieve their goals. Meet your stakeholders in person if possible or get to know them virtually.

2   Start with a meeting to outline the program goals, requirements, timeline, risks, and success measures. Then make sure their needs and expectations will be met.

3   Set up regular check-ins with these stakeholders and add them as recipients of the weekly status report.

4 If and when things that impact a stakeholder change, reach out to them to discuss the details *before* they read about them in the status report.

Bear in mind that not all stakeholders are equal. Some are more important to the program than others. Some care more about the results than others. You will spend more time with those who are more impacted. What is key is that the program manager understands how things are going and how the stakeholder is feeling about the progress of the program. Are they clear on the progress (especially when the deliverable or timeline has changed)? What has them worried? This last question can be a trigger for something that may require risk mitigation by the program manager.

For stakeholders who are impacted by the program, your job is to update them on its status, alert them to any significant issues or risks, and check in on the timing of deliverables. For more important stakeholders, this update should be timelier than waiting several days for a weekly status report. Sending a direct message or having a quick check-in meeting, virtual or otherwise, will get them up to speed right away. Even if it's just a quick check-in, when you've already built up rapport, it can be adequate time for you to deliver disappointing news and less intense for the stakeholder to hear. And that early heads-up may mean you both have more time to mitigate the impact of that news.

Regular contact with stakeholders is critical. A program manager needs to circulate and mingle with program team members, in person or virtually, so that they are aware of absolutely everything that's going on with a program, can jump on things as needed (p. 143), and can update stakeholders in a timely manner. Keep developing and maintaining effective relationships with your stakeholders, and your program management craft will thrive!

## The Role of Executive Sponsor

When a program manager is assigned to a program, usually it's because they were approached by the executive sponsor who is a senior leader responsible for getting a business goal across the line. They have decision-making authority and often have visibility at the C-level in a smaller company. At a larger company, they may have "line of business" authority. You'll know who they are as they hang around making sure things get off to a good start and are present until successful program completion.

The executive sponsor is the visionary providing the strategic direction. They sell the idea to upper management and to others around the company and create the presentation that describes the program goals. They present the program at the kickoff meeting, or perhaps at a lunch and learn, to inform others of its importance. If there's a key change to the program, they update executive leadership and get any needed approvals, and they (along with the program manager) keep key executive level stakeholders informed, preferably before the program status comes out, so that there are no surprises. The executive sponsor makes all key decisions, so if there's a proposed change to scope, schedule, or resources, they are who you talk to for approval. They are a close partner with the program manager and will attend your weekly program meetings and have weekly 1:1 meetings with you as well. Usually you have each other on speed dial as you need them and they need you just as much; they're entrusting you with their baby, as it were.

Ideally a program will have one single executive sponsor, one "throat to choke" as the saying goes. I have run programs with cosponsors, and if they communicate well and are closely aligned, this can work too. But what happens if there's no executive sponsor? First, this should sound an alarm bell. A program can't go forward without an executive sponsor who has been assigned responsibility for the effort. You should reach out to leadership to ask where the requirement for this program came from. What's the strategic level goal this program is related to? If there's no answer, then it's unlikely this work should be prioritized. Go as high up as you need to until a sponsor is assigned. If you have to, pause the work and let your manager and the leader of the organization you support know that you can't continue until you have an executive partner—or until you determine that the program isn't strategically important and should be set aside.

Program managers drive programs forward, but they do that at the request of an executive who understands the business need and is motivated to see that the work gets done. Both roles are needed for a program to be successful, and if you cultivate a healthy and tight partnership with that executive sponsor, you'll likely remain close colleagues long after the work is done.

## Business Leads as Key Partners

Building relationships with business leads is one of the key tenets of PMO methodology: the program manager should foster and nurture great business partnerships with transparent communication. That's because if program managers are the train conductor, then the business lead is in a domain specific role with specialized knowledge, for example the customer service manager or dining car specialist.

Business leads are the subject matter experts in the organization the program manager is supporting. They are required for the program to move forward. For example, where the goal of the program is to release a new product or feature, the business lead is often the product manager. For a program with the goal of supporting GDPR, the business lead is likely the general counsel (head lawyer). For a program whose goal is scalability of a software service, the business lead is likely an engineering manager or software architect. The best business leads are those who see program managers as team members and support them as they drive their programs forward. This is because both the program managers and business leads are working on behalf of the stakeholder who is expecting that their product or service is successfully delivered.

Since program managers are responsible for strategic execution, it's critical that they partner with business leads who have the domain specific expertise required for the program. The business leads work alongside program managers to keep the program team members executing on the right priorities, answer any business-related questions that crop up, make decisions that resolve an open issue, and offer solutions for effective risk mitigation.

This also means that program managers are required to have a solid understanding of the business (p. 48) to establish credibility not only with the business lead but with the whole team. The program manager should know enough to be able to understand the gist of what the business lead is talking about, what's important, and when a decision needs to be made by that business lead.

However, if the program manager isn't careful, sometimes the business lead turns over too many of the tasks mentioned above to the program manager. They begin to believe that their awesome program manager can stand in their stead and they may be conspicuously absent at meetings during which they would have been grilled about a yellow or red status. Now the program manager is thrust into the role of having to defend the team member rather than remaining objective. The business lead is no longer accountable, which means the program manager has become a crutch (p. 148).

A business lead cannot abdicate their position, and the program manager shouldn't be doing their job without the business lead/subject matter expert who has a deep understanding of the business. Program managers should make sure they know enough about the business to be effective, but they aren't and shouldn't be the business lead at the same time. As with other relationships, partnership is essential to a successful program. It's up to the program manager to nurture this relationship, to understand when to bring in the business lead, and to remain objective. When you can anticipate each other's reactions and finish each other's sentences, that's an achievement to be proud of.

## Program Manager and Functional Project Manager

Good program managers get to know all of their program
team members, especially the functional project managers on
whom they are dependent and with whom they share some
traits—and a secret handshake of sorts. The roles of program
and project manager are distinct yet closely related, and both
roles are required for a program and a company to be successful. Here's how this partnership works.

- **Program management is the process of managing multiple
  related projects working toward the same business objective.** A program is made up of several, sometimes many,
  smaller projects. For example, a program to release a new
  software product requires several engineering projects, an
  IT project for customer invoicing, a marketing project for
  launch content, and a sales project to train salespeople in
  how to sell the product.

- **Projects are domain specific and organization specific.**
  Project managers have domain specific knowledge and
  deep expertise. For example, the engineering team knows
  how to code the features, IT knows how to add that project
  to the billing system so that accounting can invoice customers, and the sales team knows how to develop sales
  training. The managers in each of these subject areas are
  known as project managers. Although project managers
  possess organizational skill sets similar to program managers, generally they are subject matter experts with deep
  expertise in a particular area. They often don't have the
  title of project manager, but you know them when you
  see them. Often they'll hold function-specific titles such

as engineering lead, IT manager, accounting lead, or marketing campaign manager.

- **Programs are strategic and cross-functional.** A program manager takes a much broader, more strategic view of the program. They depend on the functional project managers to drive and complete workstreams that ladder up to a broader program.

- **Functional project managers drive project work to completion.** They communicate start and end dates and any issues to the program manager and tend to be task-based and immersed in the granular details of a workstream. They assess cost, effort, and resourcing.

Program managers specialize in understanding just enough about all the workstreams to know how they fit together. They are also skilled in breaking down big problems into smaller chunks and helping teams determine how to get all those chunks working together at the right time. But in the end, program managers will depend on project managers to deliver their pieces of the bigger puzzle. Rest assured we don't get into the project manager's business, unless they miss a deadline or a train stop along the way!

## The Complementary Roles of Program Management and Operations

Program management is the *end-to-end* execution of programs that move a company strategy forward. There's a start and a finish to a program. The operations team is responsible for the *ongoing* people, processes, and systems that keep an organization running smoothly. So, in the context of program management, the operations team is called upon when an existing process needs to be modified to work better or a new process needs to be developed in service of a program. The operations manager, for example, might document the customer journey of trying and buying a software product, for a program with the goal of improving that journey. Program managers call on their colleagues in operations as needed to ensure program needs are met. Operations managers may dip in and out of a program or may be along for its whole lifecycle, depending on the need.

These teams share some skill sets but are primarily complementary functions when they work well together. It's important to highlight the value received when these teams work effectively together. When they are focused on similar priorities, the programs and related operational work move a company forward, and the well-run operations team ensures day-to-day functions are operating efficiently. If these functions operate in lockstep, the company benefits greatly.

An operations manager may also spearhead work that needs the help of a program manager. For example, imagine that a team would like to introduce a new tool to their arsenal, say the use of a new design tool for the creative organization. The operations manager will call on their program manager to wrap a program around that work and drive it from start to finish. The program manager will work with the IT department to validate this tooling can effectively fill a gap that no other tool can. Once they give their okay, the program manager will reach out to the security team to execute a security review. Once that passes, they interact with the procurement team in finance for funding. They work with the business lead in creative on a plan to implement and test the tool and then to put together a training session for creative team members who will be using the tool. The program manager will ensure the testing team completes their work, and once team members are successfully using the new tool, they'll hand off responsibility for tool usage and maintenance to the operations team who own the tool going forward.

Another common example is planning—long-range, annual, or quarterly. Whether doing planning at the corporate or the organizational level, operations and program management partner closely on this process. Operations owns defining and refining the planning process and often relies on program management to execute that process from end to end. Program managers share feedback with operations throughout the process so adjustments can be made as needed.

Program managers also play a role in ensuring the plans align with strategic goals. For example, C-level execs should be setting the overall direction for their organizations. That said, employees within an organization surface additional, often innovative, project ideas, and program managers ensure they are taken into account by organizational leadership who determine whether it's work that should be done or strays too far from the organizational goals and should be deprioritized. Planning is a business-critical company activity, and operations and program management should work in concert to ensure this effort is productive.

The operations and program management partnership can be summarized as follows:

- Operations ensures effective processes required for a program.

- Operations owns the ongoing people, processes, and systems that keep an organization running smoothly and brings in program management to effect end-to-end work related to process implementation. The quarterly, annual, and long-range planning processes are good examples of this partnership.

- The program manager drives programs forward, ensuring cross-functional teams are well coordinated and communicating, and brings in operations personnel if and when needed.

## The Role of the Product Manager

When the PMO at Zendesk was started, the closest role to me (in name only) was a product manager. Since the company was still small at the time, it wasn't uncommon for employees to do double duty. At that time, the product managers performed some tasks that a program manager usually handles, like setting up a program plan/schedule or driving a product launch forward. This situation is fairly common in smaller companies not yet staffed with program managers. But normally the role of the product manager is quite distinct from that of a program manager.

- Product managers represent the customer to the design and engineering teams.

- They are in regular contact with customers and understand current and future needs.

- They share knowledge with the people designing and developing products and features to drive product direction.

- They understand the competitive landscape and develop a product roadmap, weighing the importance of feature details and time to market, in the context of the company strategy.

- They foster relationships with design and engineering counterparts to ensure the right solutions are delivered at the right time to solve customer problems.

- They partner closely with a program manager who drives forward the work that needs to be completed for the customer to be satisfied.

When program managers were brought into Zendesk, they immediately filled the gap of cross-functional facilitation and coordination. They socialized the methodology of proactive strategic execution and set to work driving complex cross-functional programs forward. Except for the aforementioned few tasks the product managers or engineering leads were doing, which they quickly and happily handed over to the PMO, program managers took on the role of the objective person in the room, facilitating the sometimes heated conversations between product, engineering, and design by keeping everyone focused on the best solution for the customer.

Program managers in product development at any software company spend a lot of time with the product managers to learn what they want to accomplish on behalf of the company's customers. They spend an equal amount of time with their design and engineering counterparts to make sure they are clear on their solutions for implementing what the product manager is after. Program managers also create an open and collaborative forum in their cross-functional program meetings to facilitate communication of those customer needs and the possible implementations that will result in a successful and timely delivery to customers.

As mentioned earlier, in start-ups and smaller companies, in the absence of program management, often the product manager or technical lead may take on some of the program planning and status reporting. Although it's not ideal—doing it well requires their time and the right skill set—it can be done. What's missing is the objectivity that a program manager brings to the table, and the ability to focus full time on ensuring that the work of all the program team members will result in a successful program. Additionally, cross-functional coordination will become paramount, particularly as a company grows, and will require the full-time attention that a program manager brings to the table.

Product managers generally have good people skills since they deal with customers. That's also a required skill for program managers who are called upon to objectively facilitate a room full of team members with diverse opinions. Product managers and engineering managers alike appreciate having that neutral party in the room. As program managers become entrenched in your company, you'll probably be thankful you have each other around. Vive la différence!

## Pair Program Management

When I drove the first program at Zendesk, the PMO was a small team of two program managers. We were focused on a complex program to repackage and reprice all of the company's offerings—no small feat! Although we had divided up the work between us, it was important to have a single point of contact (POC) for program team members to reach out to for any questions or issues. We called this approach *pair program management*, and that name stuck even after we added a third program manager to the team. (We were affectionately known as PB&J after the initials of our first names.)

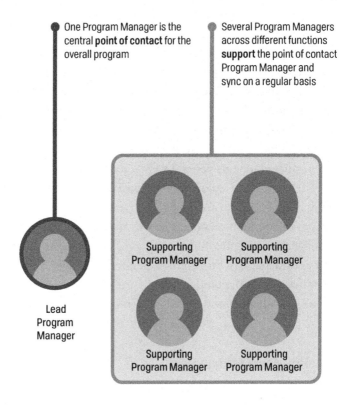

One Program Manager is the central **point of contact** for the overall program

Several Program Managers across different functions **support** the point of contact Program Manager and sync on a regular basis

Lead
Program
Manager

Supporting
Program Manager

Supporting
Program Manager

Supporting
Program Manager

Supporting
Program Manager

Pair program management requires regular communication so that the program managers across all functions keep each other up to date. The Zendesk team grew, and there are now program managers in all parts of the company; the pair program management concept is even more important.

The pair program management team does weekly syncs, usually the day before a program meeting, that might include five to six program managers (determined by the number of functional workstreams in the program). The syncs are run by the POC program manager, and the group runs in a democratic way. There may be program managers at varying levels, and often the POC is not the most senior person in the room, but they're all driving their programs in service of the larger program or portfolio. They naturally look to the POC program manager for direction and next steps. Since there is a certain amount of shared knowledge, this means that one of the pair program managers can adequately substitute for the POC program manager in case of illness or vacation. Some level of redundancy can be a good thing!

The pair program management approach is helpful throughout the program lifecycle. This team is most visible when the band gets together on "go live" day to ensure a smooth rollout, which is usually taking place simultaneously around the world. There are one or more program managers in each geographic location to make sure the rollout goes off without a hitch. Each program manager represents their functional workstream, helping to connect the dots to the broader program. That kind of support from pair program managers is welcomed by the POC program manager on what is often an exciting and stressful day.

## Key Takeaways

- Program managers must ensure that all program team members understand their role and the decisions they're expected to make during the lifecycle of a program to keeps things running smoothly.

- Regular contact between program managers and key stakeholders is critical to meeting stakeholder needs.

- Executive sponsors are the visionaries and provide the strategic direction for a program. They are partnered with the program manager who can depend on them to interact with upper management as needed.

- Program managers partner with the business lead/project manager/subject matter expert in each functional organization to ensure that workstream, which is a key part of the overall program, is successfully completed.

- Programs are cross-functional and therefore complex by nature. Many different roles are required to get a program across the line.

  o Product managers understand customer requirements and work with the team to develop solutions to customer problems.

  o Operations managers ensure effective processes are in place.

  o Functional project managers are responsible for specific functional workstreams.

- ○ Program managers bring it all home with overall coordination.

- Pair program management is a model in which a program lead responsible for a larger program or portfolio interacts with program managers across the various functions to make sure their dependent subprogram is successfully completed.

# 7

# CHECK YOUR SIGNALS

Throughout the journey of a program, there are important checkpoints and signals that you can use to determine if your program is going off track, or if it's in need of repair or improvement along the way. Well-run cross-functional program meetings with retrospectives at key milestones are useful checkpoints. Effective status reporting is also important as it signals to program team members and key stakeholders how a program is progressing, as well as what's being done about any issues or increasing risks to ensure it stays on track. This is not the time to watch the landscape roll by! Stay alert for those signals.

## Running Effective Program Team Meetings

Well-run meetings are a thing of beauty. When I was head of a PMO, I had the unique advantage of training the program managers on my team in meeting management during their onboarding. Our main meeting construct was called a program team meeting (or program meeting), and its purpose was to gather cross-functional team members together on a weekly basis. This type of cross-functional meeting is a working session to discuss the items that move a program forward. Complex cross-functional programs usually involve gathering about ten people on a weekly basis for about an hour, over several months, maybe even a year. You do the math: it's a lot of time, and time is money, and I care about operating expenses. But mostly I loathe poorly run meetings. They set my teeth on edge, and I can barely stay seated. As soon as the so-called facilitator starts to wrap up, I'm the first one out the door!

Now I admit that my standards are a little high. At one of the early Zendesk program meetings I ran, our PMO consisted of a brand-new program manager, one who was slightly more experienced, one experienced program manager on week one at the company, and me, five weeks into my new role. I was kicking off a large program and didn't yet have all of the frameworks and methodologies in place that I later established. The PMO certainly had no standard program meeting templates, and little to no expectations from the attendees, since none of them knew yet what program managers did.

I created an agenda and sent it out over email shortly before the meeting began. I felt unprepared but knew that with years of experience under my belt I would get through it. I walked through the seven agenda items so everyone knew what was to be covered. We then discussed each item and arrived at planned decisions and next steps. And we ended the meeting with five minutes to spare.

# Well-run meetings are a thing of beauty.

Back at my desk, I felt somewhat relieved to have pulled it off but vowed to be better prepared the next time. I then received a message from the product manager who had attended the meeting. He said it was the most effective meeting he had ever attended in his then five years at the company. I laughed to myself and thought, Wow, low bar! That product manager eventually left the company to travel the world, but the outlook he left behind was that program managers have a responsibility to move things forward and respect the team's valuable time in the process. So, how does a program manager do that in a program meeting? By doing the following:

- Discuss in person what can't be done (effectively) over email or direct message.

- Review the plan and what's required by whom to get to the next milestone.

- Walk through content, such as launch or performance testing plans, to get feedback.

- Bring up identified gaps or omissions and surface where alignment is needed before proceeding with the program.

- Work through issues that have surfaced and drive them to a resolution.

- Hold pre-mortems to pinpoint tasks that can be done to make sure certain problems don't happen.

- Hold retrospectives at the end of a program and at key milestones throughout. Input for that retrospective should be gathered *before* the meeting, so the meeting is a group discussion about what to start and stop, and what to do better.

One thing we definitely don't do is to go around the table and report status. This is not a status meeting—that can be done faster and more effectively over email or direct messaging.

Well-run meetings can make your team love you, but what program managers want most is an effectively run and successful program that moves the company toward its goals. That's what makes me smile as I leave the building at the end of the workday.

## Are Status Meetings Useful?

When the train conductor (program manager) is working effectively, they are always up to date on the trip progress (program status). They don't sit in their cabin for five days and then check what's going on. They're up and about, walking around, checking in with all the crew and the passengers on the train to make sure everything is going as planned. They don't need a status meeting to know where the train is headed.

Program managers are often asked, "How are things going?" They should be able to answer that question at any moment in time with an executive summary: "We're currently tracking to plan. The team is mitigating a potential scalability issue, and a response as to whether this could impact the release date is expected by the end of the workday PST."

The program manager gathers and communicates status on an ongoing basis, throughout the lifecycle of a program. Program status is best gathered by a program manager who is always checking in with team members at their (virtual) desk, over lunch or coffee, wherever team members congregate, in a 1:1 video meeting, over email, or through a direct message application such as Slack.

Meeting regularly with key stakeholders—to make sure they are happy with the program progress, update them on any changes or increasing risks, and ensure their needs haven't changed—is another way to stay in the loop. If something has changed, you will be on it. Then you can discuss the change with program team members either individually, in an impromptu meeting (if the situation is urgent), or at the weekly program meeting. Usually once a week, the program manager reports on the program status via an email update. Creating this report shouldn't take a lot of time if the program manager is up to date on what's going on.

Sometimes I see program managers fall back on gathering status in a program meeting when they haven't prepared for it. They don't have a well-thought-out agenda, and they're not up to speed on what's going on, so they just "go around the room" and each person reports on their status while the others disengage. This practice is a sign to me that the program manager is disorganized or overwhelmed (or lazy). Program managers who do not manage their time well, or do not check in regularly with team members, may be tempted to take the easy way out and just pull everyone together in a room to gather status. That's a huge waste of other people's time. Those people should be using their time together in a much more valuable way: discussing what's coming up next in the schedule, how an open issue will be resolved, or how an increasing risk will be mitigated. Next steps are assigned, and the team then gets back to work. Now you're talking!

## The Dreaded Laptop in Meetings

We've all been there. You're in a meeting and the facilitator asks a question of an attendee who looks up from their laptop with a blank stare. "I'm sorry, I wasn't listening. Could you please repeat the question?" Eye rolls and sighs ensue. At least they used the magic word, but seriously you have to wonder whether they are aware that this behavior is disrespectful of everyone in the room who was listening. This happens so much these days. People are so busy and are trying (unsuccessfully) to multitask. They arrive at a meeting, open their laptops, and start working. They look up when the meeting begins and then go right back to their (other) work. I get it: we're all overworked, overscheduled, and don't have time to stop and listen, to be fully present in a meeting. Or do we?

Program managers spend a good chunk of their time facilitating meetings and run into this circumstance often. Many program managers employ a set of practices to minimize this distracting behavior.

### 1. Do your best to make the meeting useful and productive

Review the agenda for the meeting and make sure it's a working meeting. Ask yourself these questions:

- Is the attendance of everyone required in order for the meeting to be productive?

- Do you need to discuss and solve an issue that is much more easily done with everyone in the room?

- Is a team member sharing information (new user workflow, launch plan, pricing details, etc.) that needs discussion and input?

- Is there a proposal on the table that will require lively discussion, alignment, and eventually a decision?

If you've answered yes to these questions, you're on the right track!

## 2. Check yourself

This is *not* a meeting where everyone goes around and gives status. You *never* have those meetings. That's what status reports are for, right? This is a *useful* meeting where group discussion is not optional.

## 3. Do your best to ensure active participation

You facilitate so well that you draw people into the discussion, and they are motivated to close their laptop and chime in. You know who needs to weigh in and you make sure they do. Draw out the quieter people in the meeting and give them a chance to speak. When it's time, go around the room for a verbal "I agree and commit" or "I disagree and commit."

## 4. Make sure that you have the right people in the room

One of my most naturally instinctive program managers came to me one day in frustration, worried that there were too many people in her program meeting. It had started out well enough, but after a few weeks, given the importance and visibility of the program to the company, invitations had been forwarded and the room was now full of people, most of whom weren't participating. They were there "so they didn't miss anything," but that wasn't a good use of their time. I encouraged her to cancel the meeting and start over, inviting the right people based on her RACI diagram, and making sure the meeting invite wasn't modifiable in order to limit attendees. She also added the people who were no longer included in the meeting to the status report distribution list. She got things back on track and the meeting was once again productive.

## 5. Politely ask attendees at the start of the meeting to close their laptops

I've seen this done to great effect. Some find it heavy handed but those are usually the same people who aren't listening and end up wasting everyone's time. If people feel the need to write things down, they'll bring paper and pen to future meetings. If they're a key program team member based on the RACI, they should be able to give their full attention to the meeting.

That same program manager who got her meeting back on track did these five things and ran a productive program meeting with active participation. Issues were surfaced, discussions were held, decisions were made, and next steps were assigned. However, she did have a repeat offender who would open their laptop at the start of the meeting and do other work until the meeting ended.

What should you do in this instance? Here's what that program manager did: she took the repeat offender aside after the meeting and gently suggested they need not continue to attend the meetings. Since they seemed to need time to do other work, she offered to excuse them from the meeting but made sure they received the weekly status report. She also assured them that she would contact them if they needed to weigh in on any program decisions. They agreed to the plan and were grateful to her for the time she saved them. This repeat offender also got the message—for any future meetings of hers they did attend, they were fully present.

## Running Retrospectives

Post-mortems, known as retrospectives in today's agile world, are an important activity for program managers to run not only at the end of a program but also after key milestones. Identifying ways to improve execution before, during, and at the end of a program simply makes good sense in this increasingly dynamic world.

The whole point of a retrospective is to review three things:

1 What went well

2 What didn't go well

3 What actions could improve the process going forward

According to Scrum.org, retrospectives can and should be done at the completion of each sprint, which usually has a duration of two weeks. In a broader, complex program, a program manager should run the retrospective as appropriate throughout its lifecycle.

When I worked at Zendesk, all program managers ran retrospectives at the completion of a program. Increasingly, they started a program with a pre-mortem exercise where the program team imagines that the program has failed and then works backward to determine what potentially could cause it to fail, reviews each threat, and takes preventive actions.

For longer or more complex programs, program managers work with their executive sponsor and/or business leads to insert retrospectives at key points in the program. Improvements are made along the way, which saves time and allows the program team members to adjust plans and/or process to what's going on, even if it only matters the next time around. If they wait until the end of the program, they often have forgotten some of the things that happened months earlier.

Program retrospectives are held with all program team members (cross-functional representatives) and program stakeholders present. If everyone is physically present in the same room, the whiteboard is a great place for gathering feedback. But in today's increasingly virtual world, so many programs involve several geographies, and more and more people working from home; virtual whiteboards have become a popular tool.

Another strategy is to use a shared spreadsheet where participants enter their information in real time and the program manager organizes the data by topic area, also in real time. In a block of time at the end of the meeting, the program manager leads everyone through key points, or potential changes in the way the program team functions, that are up for discussion. It may help to send out a link to a shared spreadsheet prior to the retrospective, allowing program team members time to think through their feedback and enter it. Then the program manager reviews it prior to the meeting, organizes it by topic area, surfaces the salient points, and summarizes what went well, what didn't, and what they will improve going forward.

No one wants to repeat the same mistakes. In today's dynamic world, where it's almost expected that the best laid plans will change, retrospectives are a great tool for program managers to ensure the program will indeed meet its goals, especially if they're changing as you go.

## Green, Yellow, Red

Status reporting is key to keeping program stakeholders in the loop, and it allows them to react to changes in a timely manner. Formal communication is typically done via status reporting. Early on in a program, you might report status on a biweekly basis, but as the program progresses, reports will likely come out weekly.

So how does the magic happen? At the end of each week, a program manager steps back and reviews the overall program goals and metrics, checks in on progress to plan, reviews open issues and increasing risks, and determines if a program is:

- GREEN: on track

- YELLOW: at risk and mitigating

- RED: blocked or not likely to get back on track without intervention

Sometimes team members may view a yellow or red status as a bad mark, a sign to leadership that they are not doing their jobs. This couldn't be further from the truth. Sh*t happens! Even with carefully laid plans, a wrench can get thrown into a program. Perhaps an acquisition changes the scope of the program, or company priorities shift due to competitive pressure, or a key resource departs unexpectedly. The program manager must accurately represent program status and they should explain in the report why the status is flagged yellow or red, what the team is doing about it, and when they expect to be back to green.

I suggest using a data-driven approach wherever possible, but the program manager should also work in their assessment of the overall health of the program. Objectivity plays an important part in how program managers do their job (p. 199) and that holds here as well, as the ultimate goal is for the program manager to communicate accurate status of the program to key stakeholders. There are tools that automatically calculate the status of a program based on a collection of data, for example, achieving milestones on schedule or how long an issue has been open. Whether status is calculated automatically or by hand, the purpose of these status colors is to convey to key stakeholders how things are progressing so that expectations are correctly set.

A best practice for a program manager is to alert a program team member whose team is responsible for a status change (whether the status is changing from green to yellow or yellow to red) that the status is about to be sent out. This gives the team member time to alert their functional leadership about the status change and the details surrounding it. It's also important to word the change in status in a way that is fact based and avoids finger pointing. The reason for the delay is clear and, more importantly, the work in progress to get the status back to green is included. Writing status reports objectively and alerting your team members ahead of time that the news is about to land means they won't feel you've thrown them under the bus.

Additionally, if a program stakeholder is given enough notice that something that affects them has changed, they can react more capably (and this is the responsibility of the program manager and/or executive sponsor). When they don't find out until the last minute because the team was hoping to find a solution, the stakeholder is left holding the bag. Teams shouldn't be afraid to have their program manager report on a yellow or red status as the program progresses. Stakeholders, and leadership, understand that there will be ups and downs and that things won't always be flagged green. As long as the team is mitigating, a yellow or red status is not a black eye. The exception to this is if the same mistake is repeated. Then get ready for questions.

Team members should trust that the program manager has their eye on the program goal(s) at all times and will report objectively on status. A good program manager will never (ever) be swayed by a team member wanting to cover up what's going on to make the team look good. A well-functioning team will have established a high level of trust and smooth communication between team members and the program manager, which means no one is surprised by a status report. And that's a wonderful thing! Accurate status reports are to be celebrated rather than feared.

## A Second Pair of Eyes

Status reports may take several hours for a program manager to write because they are time-consuming and tricky. The program manager must step back and reflect on how things are going, compare progress to plan, and check in with team members or dependent teams to confirm details as often as necessary. The goal is to determine the most important things for the reader to take away, so clear, concise, accurate status is of the utmost importance. Status reporting is hard to do well because the program manager must objectively and clearly report status on problems, but they shouldn't throw anyone under the bus. Needless to say, a careful review by a PMO colleague to catch any errors keeps misinformation from being spread.

I recommend that all program managers have a program management colleague review their status report prior to emailing it to a broad audience. The reviewer should use an agreed upon checklist and general guidelines as they verify that the status color is accurate, milestones are updated, and explanations are clear. Sometimes a program manager is so well versed in the details that an acronym or an explanation is clear to them, but it is opaque to potential readers, which includes everyone in the program RACI matrix (p. 102).

Occasionally a program manager believes they've reported a situation objectively, but the reviewer might notice that's not the case. Believe me, I've seen relief on the face of a program manager when their reviewer catches something like this. This kind of course correction prevents the program manager from spending days or weeks repairing a relationship with someone whose work situation was misrepresented.

A shorter status report is usually a good thing if you're trying to get people to read it and internalize it. When a status report is too full of detail, the reader may miss key content. Stakeholders can miss an issue that requires their attention.

I've seen milestone dates reported inaccurately (the wrong day or month), sometimes due to a simple typo. Think of the time saved by catching that before it goes out and several people repeat it and stakeholders become unnecessarily alarmed. Errors that would otherwise be just plain embarrassing (such as typos, grammatical issues, and broken links) are easily caught by a reviewer. They are pretty common (hey, we're all human!) and much easier to spot with a second pair of eyes. I read all of the status reports my team members send out and I can quickly tell who skipped a review in the interest of time, or thought that they didn't need anyone to check their work. Status reports are often the only examples stakeholders see of a program manager's work so it's important that you make a good impression. You and your readers will be glad you did.

### No Notes Please!

Now, I have yet to say anything about note taking, and by that, I mean taking down the minutes of a meeting. Notes usually include everything that has happened already, rather than what's ahead. So, although I encourage documenting decisions and noting next steps, along with who's assigned to each, that's about it for the notes a program manager needs from a meeting. As I mentioned earlier, it's best for someone else to be writing down these notes because note taking gets in the way of the program manager's actual job.

Wouldn't you rather have your program manager focused on effectively facilitating the meeting, moving the meeting along in a timely way, observing facial expressions that might indicate a question, lack of alignment, or disagreement? Or would you rather they miss those important cues, let someone hijack the meeting, go down a rabbit hole, and leave the attendees wondering what was accomplished because the program manager was too fixated on taking accurate notes? I'd much rather know that the team left the meeting clear on action items and key decisions.

Now, I will admit that I'm not a habitual notetaker, but some program managers, engineers, product managers, and executives are. I had a manager, the former COO of Zendesk, who liked to handwrite in a notebook during meetings because it helped him commit key items to memory. Write things down if it works for you. But the program manager should never think it's their *job* to note down everything that's being said in a meeting they are facilitating. Instead I encourage you to focus on what matters: making sure the meeting objectives are met in order to drive the program forward, and noticing if an issue is surfacing or a risk is increasing so you can determine a mitigation plan.

And please *never* take notes for someone else's meeting! I have a few ways to deal with requests to do this. My favorite response is to say politely that I'm not in a position to do that, but I'm sure [insert name of another colleague in the room] would be willing to step up. That usually does the trick. To avoid repeated requests, don't bring your laptop to a meeting you're not facilitating, then you won't be asked. If you are facilitating and someone asks who's writing things down, gently suggest that if they feel notes are important, they might consider taking on the task. After all, the average professional can type!

One final suggestion: a program manager at Zendesk has a super effective way of dealing with the notes situation. He liked to open a shared document at the start of the meeting that contained the agenda. When a next step was agreed upon, or a decision was made, he would ask the person involved to please type that into the shared doc. He found that kept everyone engaged in the meeting and it also increased accountability. Given that he was often facilitating people in a room with him as well as several remote locations on screen, with this approach he was able to stay focused on the goals for the meeting and also keep his eyes on the attendees (harder than it looks!). He rarely missed a grimace, an eye roll, or a smirk!

## Key Takeaways

- Effective program meetings focus on upcoming milestones, open issues, increasing risks, and gathering alignment as the program moves forward.

- The program manager should spend time with the team they support throughout the work week in order to gather status rather than doing it in a meeting.

- Limit laptop use by meeting participants so that you don't have to repeat yourself because someone is not paying attention to the discussion.

- Running retrospectives during a program allows program team members to course correct as needed. Retrospectives at the end of a program are a good way to make sure future programs run more effectively.

- When you flag items green, yellow, or red in a status report, this allows team members, leadership, and stakeholders to know how a program is progressing and if expectations are set correctly.

- Ask a PMO colleague to review your status report before it goes out to ensure it's clear, accurate, and doesn't single out a person or a team unfairly.

- Avoid taking notes in a program meeting so you can focus instead on what's coming next in the program and what's being said (or not). Keep your eyes on the participants to ensure alignment.

# 8

# WHEN SIGNALS
# GET CROSSED

—◯—

In the last few chapters, I've talked about the key skills
program managers need to set up a program for success,
how to develop and nurture key relationships, and how
to keep everyone informed around program status by using
certain signals to highlight areas that need work. Sometimes
those signals get crossed. That's when you need some best
practices to rectify the situation, clear the tracks ahead, and
keep the train running smoothly and on time.

## The Program Manager Mingle

Getting out among your program team members and building
relationships is critical to your success as a program manager.
Program managers drive complex cross-functional programs
that advance the company goals, which are usually set on an
annual basis within the context of the long-term company
strategy. As I've said earlier, program managers do what is

Getting out among your program team members is critical to program success.

called strategic execution, and I've designed a proactive framework for program managers that ensures success:

- Meet (in person or virtually) with team members to work through issues in a timely manner and check in to find out how the program is progressing.

- Connect with dependent teams to ensure their work is going to plan and will be delivered on time.

- Sync with stakeholders to confirm the program is meeting their needs.

- Work with program team members to drive open issues to resolution.

- Mitigate risks that are increasing or uncover new ones you need to keep an eye on.

None of this requires that a program manager be hunkered down at their desk. They are not writing code, a product plan, or a requirements document that requires quiet, focused time away from others. They may periodically update a program plan or a risk register but that should take a few minutes, although writing a status report can take a couple of hours once a week.

If you are running a program, you need to be spending a generous amount of time with your program team, in person or virtually. If you are a PMO leader, it's important that you get around on a regular basis to wherever your program managers hang out to ensure this is happening and provide coaching if not. This may require traveling to spend time with program managers supporting teams located around the world. I like to observe the working styles of program managers on my team so I can tell if they are communicating effectively with their teams. I also observe whether their team members are coming to find them to chat through an issue or brainstorm with them about a new way to think about an aspect of the program. When I see program managers meeting with their functional team leads formally or informally, or huddling with their fellow program managers responsible for the dependent parts of their program, that's all good stuff.

But if a program manager is spending an inordinate amount of time on their own, this sends the wrong signal to me and to their team members. If the program manager isn't making an effort to spend time with the organization they support, that speaks volumes. If a key stakeholder tells me, "I never see Jorge!" I reach out to that person's manager to find out what's going on. Why aren't they visible to their team? Why aren't they making themselves available in case an issue is bubbling up?

Whether you're a people person or more of an introvert, the job of program manager requires you to spend time (in person or virtually) with your colleagues, building or nurturing important relationships, keeping your ear to the ground for issues, and generally being a good team member to your program team and stakeholders. Your manager is watching where and how you spend your time, as are your program team and stakeholders, so get out (or online) and mingle!

## Seeing Is Believing

Once I was invited to an organization's all hands meeting where the group was trying to figure out how to scale to meet the needs of the teams they service. As the facilitator brought me into the conversation and I began offering ideas, the organization's leader expressed concern that somehow his role and mine would overlap. I could see that he didn't understand the role of the PMO, but since he wanted my team to engage, I knew he was open to partnering with us. Fast-forward several months, we were in a program meeting and I had helped to unblock the team to move forward on their key initiative. That same leader said, "Ah, I get it now. Program management drives big things forward." Yup, that's about the size of it!

Building out the PMO at Zendesk taught me many things. But one lesson that continues to resonate is that occasionally people don't know they need program management until they see it in action. To quote Rod Tidwell (or Cameron Crowe), "Show me the money!" When someone says this, they either want to know how much they will be paid for something or want to see evidence that something is worth paying for. Program management can be like that. You don't know you need it. You're not sure you want to invest in it. You finally do and, without fail, you say several weeks or months later that you "can't imagine life without program management!" You see the value add and are glad you invested the headcount in program management.

Over my career, I've received all kinds of requests for support. Some are direct. They get it. They want it. Great! Those are the easy ones. Some are less clear. The request sounds more like, "So I've been told I need to include program management on this initiative." Hey, that's good enough for me to at least engage with the requester. That's because I'm confident in a program manager's ability to add value, something that you can ensure through proper hiring and onboarding, focusing on the most important issues for the organization, developing a methodology or playbook for driving programs forward, and partnering effectively with your stakeholders.

But sometimes people are so tentative about how program management can work for them that they need a little more time to truly understand it. For instance, buoyed by the overwhelmingly positive impact of a recently hired program manager, one team asked for some additional help. Unfortunately, that request didn't come with an additional headcount, and we were up to our ears in work. They then asked if we could just provide some meeting management basics and some schedule templates, and they'd take on those programs themselves. Okay... sure. We'll just wave the program management wand and poof, you're a program manager! Well, we put aside our bruised egos and provided them a few tools as requested, and even spent a bit of time helping them kickstart the programs. A few weeks later, they came back to us. "So yeah, this is harder than it looks." They had seen program management in action, and it was so effective that they became true believers (okay, after trying it themselves first!) and began discussing additional headcount. Talented program managers who are highly skilled at the discipline make their job look easy. Showing what we do is often more effective than talking about it.

## Program Management as a Crutch

How do you avoid the trap of fixing (or trying to fix) everyone and everything simply because you are asked and because you can? Well, the best way I know is to concentrate on the tasks that a program manager does best and which no one else can do. Sure, a program manager supporting the marketing team has seen enough campaign schedules that they can draft one. But the subject matter expert can do this better than a program manager who should be spending time on cross-functional coordination—something no one else can do. Program managers drive forward complex cross-functional *programs* and this requires a skilled individual. *Projects*, which are organization or domain specific, don't require a program manager's skill set to move them forward and should *not* have a program manager assigned to them. Subject matter experts in the organization are actually the project managers (p. 15). They are able to run these projects themselves and should. The projects will likely be associated with or ladder up to a program in progress. But these projects should not be run by a program manager because this will:

- **Create dependency:** If a program manager provides too much assistance, then an organization may become dependent on them to run even the smallest project. This is not financially sound, as there are never enough program managers to run all projects in an organization as well as the larger, more complex cross-functional programs.

- **Undermine professional development:** Program managers don't want to create an organization full of leaders/managers who can't run their own projects. The leaders should possess the skills required to run projects and develop them to be an all-around professional. For example, every professional businessperson should know how to run an effective project meeting, create a project schedule, and deliver that work on time.

- **Weaken accountability:** Business leads will no longer be accountable for their own work. They can't be allowed to opt out of their responsibilities. They're the subject matter experts and need to pull their weight and do the work expected of them by the program team.

Program managers are experts at running meetings and creating schedules, of course, but their time is better spent doing what they are best at: strategic execution. Said another way, they're the best and only person to run a big, complex cross-functional program meeting or to create a complex schedule with many interdependencies. If a company can free up its program manager to be even more effective, focusing on the things only they can do, and can ensure the functional teams step up and own the work that is domain specific, teams will run more efficiently and you'll have happy program managers.

## When the Train Has Left the Station

When I worked at Zendesk, a program manager told me how much he enjoyed a recent blog post of mine called "Program Managers as Train Conductors" (p. 42). This compliment was followed by an awkward pause and shuffling of feet. "Yes?" I said. "That's all well and good," he said. I could feel the "but" coming. "But the train has already left the station and I feel like I'm running after it and I'm not sure it's headed in the right direction!" Ruh-roh! I think but don't say. Instead I followed with an encouraging "You've got this!"

He did, actually. He's a talented program manager with great instincts. He described what he was doing to catch the train: review the remaining trip itinerary and either keep going or slow the train to rethink the plan and get things back on track. He was describing a situation that program managers face more often than not: he was brought on board only after the trip was in progress.

Catching a moving train requires that you accelerate the usual program start-up process (p. 76). The first thing to do is quickly ascertain how far the train has already traveled and what work has been done. Then once you've managed to jump on board, it's important to ask questions similar to those you would have asked at the start:

- What's the problem you're (already) trying to solve?

- How will this work (you've already started) to move the company goals forward?

- Is everything going well now? Or is it time to reorient the train, switching tracks if necessary to avoid wasting additional effort?

It can be hard to jump on board a moving train, let alone stop one. A lot of discovery and investigation work may have already been done, and implementation may have begun. But if you're solving the wrong problem, those miles traveled will be wasted anyway and there's no sense in continuing down the wrong track. However, the program manager may need to use all the negotiating skills they have to put the brakes on the program and backtrack.

The team might push back, but you can encourage them to gather data to prove that their itinerary is the right one. Since you are an objective program manager, your opinion isn't what matters here. Your goal is simply to focus the team on the right problem and the work that will provide the right solution for the customer. Do some rediscovery until you are sure the chosen path is the right one, or you need to stop at the next station and switch tracks to go in the right direction. Myriad reasons exist for needing to slow or halt the train: a requested change in direction from management, competitive pressure, or a reassessment of customer needs. Everyone will need to disembark, taking their luggage with them. It's frustrating to have to start over or backtrack and throw away work that's no longer relevant. But continuing in the wrong direction is definitely worse.

While the train is slowed, or stopped, this is a good time to ask about success measures, particularly if things are changing. What are the expectations when the train arrives at its destination? Does a feature need to arrive on a certain date? That's certainly a worthy and quite measurable goal. However, the real measure of success might be validating that customers enjoyed the ride (i.e., they have started using the feature) and that the company has solved their problem.

Slowing or stopping the train and redirecting efforts requires that program managers play the important role of change manager: facilitating the team through change and getting the train moving again in the right direction with the right people on board. Halting a moving train is never fun! But once things get going in the right direction, the team will thank you. Time for drinks in the bar car!

It's hard to stop a moving train, but if you're solving the wrong problem, the distance traveled will be wasted.

## Just When You Think You Have a Plan

Just when you think plans are finalized, and the programs for the organization you support are humming along, a wrench is thrown into the plans, often a request for additional program support. A new priority has surfaced and someone from the organization you're supporting says, "I need a program manager, stat!" Ah, if only it was that simple! What this request usually requires is a completely new program or set of workstreams that will require not only a program manager but resources from team members already assigned to other programs. And often the new program or set of workstreams will require resources from downstream organizations such as IT or marketing.

The first thing to consider is who's asking and determine why this request is important. As a team, you'll need to decide if the request is more important than the work the team is already assigned to. Ask these questions before you proceed:

- Is this request in support of the company goals?

- Is it important enough that something should be bumped down the priority list?

- What work will be delayed if we take on this new request?

- Could the scope of an existing program be reduced to make this request happen?

- Are there underutilized resources that could be applied to this request?

After you've worked your way through these questions, more often than not the requester will realize that this work can wait until resources are freed up. But sometimes the team's and the program's priorities must shift. The worst-case scenario is that more work will be added to the pile. If that's the case, the program manager should gather the team to gauge the impact of adding this work to what they're already doing. The program manager will surface the impact of the additional work to the appropriate leadership for approval.

Although program managers don't make prioritization decisions, they do translate the request for support from a problem into a proposed solution and its impact. Then they enlist the leadership team for the organization they support to review the request and align everyone and determine next steps. Once a decision is made, the program manager, with assistance from the executive sponsor if needed, takes care of the appropriate communications to the program team members, key stakeholders, and leadership. If plans are adjusted, those changes are recorded for posterity: it can be useful at the next retrospective to review why a change was made and discuss how to improve things the next time around.

Like they say, the only constant is change. The important thing is that the program manager effectively manages that change with their program team and functional leadership to meet company goals.

## Taking a Spring Break

Spring break at North American universities is a time-honored tradition. It gives students time to relax and recharge before they finish up the school year. When I attended university in New York State, spring break meant a twenty-four-hour drive to Miami, the most popular destination for some fun in the sun. So what does this have to do with program management? Sometimes a break in the middle of a long program can be just the ticket for the team.

I once participated as executive sponsor for a long, complex, necessary, and decidedly un-glamorous program run by a very skilled program manager. The work centered on the need to migrate customers from several earlier versions of software to the most recent one. (Trust me, the work was challenging and interesting in a nerdy sort of way!) The team could see beyond the program to a better and more beautifully simple world for customers and their users. That goal was enough to keep us motivated over the long haul, which stretched eighteen months before all was said and done.

The program manager ran the program from the company's Singapore office, and team members were located there, in Melbourne, and in San Francisco. This meant weekly program meetings late in the day for those of us in San Francisco and early in the morning for the APAC team members. Besides the weekly program meetings, there were countless other meetings between engineers and product managers across these same three geographies. But the program manager deftly facilitated across the digital divide, ensuring progress, building relationships, and creating a wonderful virtual camaraderie I had not experienced before or since.

Unfortunately, about nine months into the program, we ran into a technical roadblock caused by a neighboring team with an unforeseen dependency that meant a delay and some head-scratching by that dependent team. The program manager sensed that continuing to move forward wasn't going to be a productive use of the program team's time, so he suggested we take a "spring break" to let the dependent team catch up. Now this didn't mean we hit the clubs and worked on our tan. We put our work on hold for a few weeks while the dependent team completed their related work. The program team members appreciated the chance to shift focus and work on something different and, in some cases, less time critical. All of us returned to the program refreshed, renewed, and ready to complete the final months of the program.

The program was successfully completed, although it did require some clever deployment strategies and some nail-biting to get the code deployed before the holiday production freeze. On the "go live" day, when the last code was live and tests completed to our satisfaction, the team unanimously asked the program manager to give a congratulatory speech. Since program managers are usually working quietly in the background, this request highlighted the leadership and foresight he demonstrated throughout the program. The team spirit he cultivated throughout the long months was deeply valued by the entire team—he was their guru. Spring break was a good call on his part and is a strategy you might consider if you find yourself and your team in a similar situation.

## When to Walk Away

Taking a break is one great tactic to move a program forward in a productive way, but sometimes the best solution is to walk away, something I never do lightly. I once got involved in a program that the PMO was not yet supporting but desperately needed a course correction. I was called in to help and did my level best to get things back on track. Unfortunately, that assistance was viewed by one of the business leads as prolonging the effort, so reluctantly I stepped away even though I and the other team members knew that continuing down the same path the program was on would, and did, cause it to fail. At that point, with the business lead in question now sidelined, program management was asked to step back in. The program was course corrected and successfully completed, finally meeting customer needs but not without considerable delay.

Program managers are the bridge over the cross-functional gaps that exist in most organizations. They bring people together, working to create alignment where diverse opinions exist and mediating disagreements; they facilitate and negotiate effectively. Program managers get involved in a program when there is a problem to solve or a business objective to meet, one that's complex and cross-functional.

Most of the time the team welcomes a program manager's involvement. Occasionally they are reluctant and are directed to ask for our involvement. After a few weeks of working with us, they see the value of program management and get quickly on board. However, once in a while, a team member asks for our help, the PMO gets things up and running, but later the team member wants to do things their own way. Now we have a problem. We want to help—and we know we can— but there's a roadblock.

A lack of collaboration may manifest in a team member's refusal to provide milestones (p. 78), show up for important meetings, or meet commitments. This issue is usually best addressed by the program manager connecting with the uncooperative team member to find out what's going on.

Perhaps they are under pressure from their manager to go in a direction that doesn't align with program objectives.

But it's also possible they are a lone wolf and are no longer willing to collaborate with the broader team. In that situation, I recommend the program manager calmly point out the benefits to cross-functional collaboration (there's no *i* in team) and encourage the team member to rejoin the effort. This process may go on for a few days, weeks, or maybe even months. But we program managers don't give up easily as it's our nature to bring people together.

If the program manager has used all the tools in their tool belt (p. 170) to persuade the team member to collaborate, then the program manager should reach out to this person's manager. Hopefully the program manager has the support of their own manager during this process, and they may also seek support and advice from others in the PMO. When one of my program managers is in this awkward situation, I make it clear that I have their back and will encourage them to stick it out if possible. But at some point, the program manager may need to accept that this particular individual just isn't a team player. The program manager will need to let that difficult team member go it alone, and cross their fingers that all turns out well.

If you have to step away from a program, this is best done after a key milestone is met, or a key phase of a multi-phase program is completed. Then things can be handed over in a friendly and professional way, with the proviso that if the team wants the involvement of the PMO in the future, they shouldn't hesitate to reach out. If they do come back for help, take a hard look to make sure that difficult team member has turned the page and their manager is on board to ensure their collaboration throughout the program. Program manager personalities are such that they generally don't indulge in schadenfreude—they don't want to see anyone fail even if an individual has proved challenging to work with. But if someone repeatedly refuses the help of a program manager, you should be ready to walk away. Program managers always have plenty of other requests for their expertise!

## Getting Together to Move Forward

I remember a program manager at Adobe who was working on a tricky upgrade of an internal tool used by a department in another geographic region. Technical struggles dragged on for a few weeks, and bad feelings had surfaced across the ocean. Instead of throwing up her hands and walking away, she dug in and employed another tactic. Given that the team members had never actually met in person, she got support from management to fly the team to one location. The first day was supremely awkward because cross words had been exchanged prior to the face-to-face meeting. But everyone made up over a welcome dinner and got to know each other as people. The program manager happily reported, "We actually became friends by the end of the week!" From then on, despite the miles that separated the team members, technical problems were worked through speedily.

In today's global economy, many of our program teams are made up of people from several different geographies, which can present some issues and risks as discussed in Chapter Five. One solution to this conundrum is to get the entire team together in the same location periodically—it can make a world of difference.

Early on in the creation of the PMO at Zendesk, we had engineering teams located in five different geographies. Now combine that geographic complexity with a big cross-functional program and you have one of the reasons the Program Management Office (PMO) was formed in the first place. For program managers, teams spread across multiple locations means finding a meeting time that works for everyone so team members can be in the same virtual room on a weekly, biweekly, or monthly basis, depending on what's appropriate. These virtual meetings are helpful, but more is needed.

Gathering the team together in one physical location, often at the start of a big program, can pay huge dividends. This kind of gathering can be a kickoff, or an alignment on requirements. For multi-phase programs, the team may gather in person to kick off each successive phase of work. But even if the team meets only once in person for a program, you'll reap the rewards several months later when those employees are working through a difficult problem.

When I worked at Adobe, I drove a program that had two engineering teams in the US, one on the West Coast and one on the East. The teams were talking, got along well, and there was only a three-hour time difference, but the code was just not coming together. Deadlines were approaching and the pressure was increasing, so we flew one team out to work with the other. Within a couple of days, a solution was found for work that had dragged on for months and we got back on schedule. Lack of clarity up-front had the teams working at cross-purposes,  and they didn't realize it until they were all in the same physical room.

But what happens if travel isn't possible? Limited budget, personal constraints, a worldwide pandemic—these are some reasons travel might be restricted. If in-person gatherings must be replaced by virtual ones, check out my tips on making this as productive as possible (p. 94). If your teams are lucky enough that travel is possible, these kinds of trips are invaluable. But whether in person or virtual, as program managers, it's your task to make these gatherings effective. Work with your teams to define clear goals up-front, get the right people in the room (minus those wanting to tag along for a free trip), create a detailed agenda, and document desired outcomes for each session before the gathering begins. Your teams may initially grumble at the structure, but they'll thank you in the end. Pack your bags!

## Key Takeaways

- Mingle with your team members and stakeholders to know what's really going on, so you can mitigate risks or learn about new ones and keep in touch with changing stakeholder requirements.

- Some people don't know they need program management until they see it in action.

- Avoid the trap of fixing everyone and everything just because you are asked and you can. Focus on strategic execution and leave projects to the business team with the subject matter expertise to ensure accountability.

- Jumping into a program in progress is challenging because stopping work or backtracking is often met with resistance. But there's no sense in continuing down the same track if you're solving the wrong problem!

- Change is constant. A program manager effectively manages that change with their program team and leadership to achieve company goals.

- Sometimes taking a spring break during a long program is a good thing.

- Know when to walk away, if someone doesn't want the help of a program manager or is uncooperative.

- Getting the team together periodically in the same location builds collaboration and helps solve intractable problems.

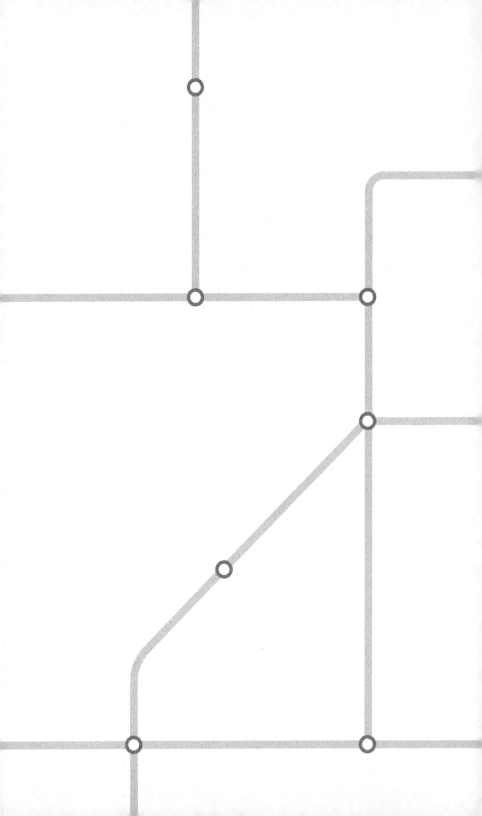

# PART THREE

# LEVELING UP YOUR PROGRAM MANAGEMENT SKILLS

# 9

# YOU NEED MORE
# THAN A WHISTLE

—O—

Along the way, I've talked about some of the skills that a program manager must have, including the ability to plan and schedule, to mitigate risks and close issues to keep a program on track, to effectively communicate status, and to educate yourself about the business of the teams you support. But to ensure the train arrives on time and with the right things on board, you'll need more than just your whistle! It's the soft skills—or superpowers, as I like to call them—that make the difference between a good and a great program manager. This topic is probably one of my favorite things to talk about, and this chapter explores the superpowers that make great program managers and PMO leaders and identifies what you should look for when interviewing and hiring prospective candidates, as well as covers onboarding and professional development.

When I select program manager candidates, I look for a certain set of hard skills and experience. Many candidates come with relevant experience and that experience gets them in the door for the interview. I ask questions to determine past behavior by focusing on situations that a program manager will face in order to assess if they are the right fit for the dynamics of the job.

But it's most important for me to figure out if the candidate has the soft skills or superpowers required to be a program manager who excels at their job. Superpowers like getting someone to do something they don't want to do or helping someone solve a problem or being comfortable working behind the scenes to make things happen. They might tell you a story about how good they felt when they got a program across the line. If I ask the candidate if anyone thanked them, a good program manager will look puzzled and explain that they get satisfaction from seeing the program completed successfully. Bingo!

An individual who takes time to get to know a person and has the patience to communicate well is more likely to be successful in getting a team member on board with a plan. You have to lay out the pros and cons and appeal to their sense of doing what's right for the team and the program. And yes, sometimes this means playing to their ego. For that, you need to be cool and collected, and not everyone has access to that pool of calm. You can teach someone how to build a timeline or how to set up a risk register, but you can't always teach someone to be unemotional if that's who they are naturally. Training someone to be empathetic, to care about others' problems is challenging. Without these superpowers, a candidate simply won't make a great program manager.

So next time you're hiring for a program manager, once you've established that they have the core skills to do the job, suss out whether they have these superpowers so that you hire the right individual for the role.

# Harness your superpowers for excellence.

## The Program Manager's Tool Belt

I've always been a visual learner, so when I think about the soft skills/superpowers that I look for in a program manager, I have a visual in my head of a person with a tool belt, just like the leather one my dad wore when doing construction projects around the house. Although he spent his career as a software professional and a university professor, my father was the son of a cabinet maker and spent many of his weekends building things around the house.

Today, whenever I talk with a program management leader about a particular development area for one of their program managers, I picture that program manager adding a tool to their belt of program management skills. The goal is to fill that belt with a variety of tools so that they can pull out the right tool for the situation at hand. Here is the list of skills and attributes I look for when interviewing prospective program managers, followed by a description of why I think each of these is important.

- Super organized
- Proactive
- Strategic thinker
- Detail oriented
- Clear and concise communicator
- Relationship builder
- Rallies consensus
- Influences without authority
- Analytical
- Even-keeled temperament
- Supportive
- Good listener
- Empathetic
- Enjoys working behind the scenes

## Super organized

At the top of my list is good organizational skills. Is your desktop neat and tidy? Is your cable drawer a well-organized, neatly labeled thing of beauty that would make Marie Kondo weep? Then you probably have one of the most powerful superpowers a program manager needs.

When you are hiring program managers, it's crucial to assess the organizational skills of the candidates. If you're an individual contributor (IC) program manager, much of what you are doing is organizing others to get a program across the line. You create the plan and then you execute it, making sure the right people are on board the train at the right time. A good program manager is always thinking about the next few milestones in the plan and how they will get the team there. They think about the requirements for each milestone, who needs to be involved, and what they need to do, leaving nothing to chance. And that's the reason why the first program manager tool is being super organized. It's a skill akin to a hammer and nails in a tool belt—essential and versatile.

## Proactive

This skill is the biggest game changer when it comes to adding value to the teams you support as a program manager. By this point in the book, you know that my approach to program management is proactive (as opposed to a lean-back approach where you wait for the team to contact you). The PMO is a services organization, and the program manager's role is to understand the strategic context of the teams you support and to partner closely with them on a set of programs that achieve the team's desired outcomes. This requires you as program manager to lean in and learn all you can, reaching out to your teams and stakeholders to build relationships, and understanding risks and proactively mitigating each and every one in the drive forward to reach the team's goals. In your tool belt, this is your spring tool—you know, "spring forward"!

## Strategic thinker

Program managers need to be strategic thinkers so that they understand the context in which they are operating. This helps them effectively prioritize the initiatives of the teams they support. I liken this skill to a flashlight, because you need to see the dark forest beyond the trees in front of you. To determine, for example, if an urgent request for program management serves the strategy of the organization you support such that ongoing work should be deprioritized to make room for the new request. Sometimes you'll find the requester is only considering the needs of their own team (the trees) and not the broader organization (the forest) in which case your strategic thinking flashlight will help establish key priorities and reset their expectations.

## Detail oriented

Not only is it crucial for a program manager to be strategic and see the big picture, they also need to be detail oriented. They're running complex programs and they need to understand the technical details enough to know when something is an issue. They need to have a good handle on the detailed program plan and interdependencies. You've now added a magnifying glass to your tool belt.

### Clear and concise communicator

Program managers should also be able to communicate clearly and concisely, which is important when providing verbal or written status updates to management, team members, and key stakeholders. This individual is interested in productive conversation, open communication, and a free flow of information. In a meeting setting, a program manager will announce a topic for discussion and kick things off but then encourage others to speak. They keep a close watch on how the conversation is progressing and won't let it spiral out of control. They are comfortable taking a back seat in support of open communication and leaning back in as needed to assert control to get the conversation back on track. Now you've added a carpenter's pencil to your growing arsenal of tools.

### Relationship builder

Program managers need to understand the importance of building relationships such that they can lean on their colleagues to get work done (without micro-managing) and still be friends afterward. This involves spending time with your colleagues to get to know them both professionally and personally. If a colleague is struggling, you'll want them to trust you and share their difficulty with you, so you can jump in and get them the help they need. You know that tape measure you loved to play with as a kid? You'd pull it way out and then let it snap back into place, and then do it ten or twenty more times until your dad said with exasperation, "That's not a toy!"? Well, I'm not sure if this metaphor works, but that tape measure is still fun—and it's an important tool!

### Rallies consensus

Programs are usually complex cross-functional initiatives that don't move forward without a talented program manager. These programs often involve varying and competing priorities, so the ability to rally consensus from a large group of diverse stakeholders in a pleasant and non-threatening way is critical. This skill involves reminding the group of the program goals or the train destination, if you will. You need to steer them away from their personal opinions or what would be easiest for their team by highlighting why the program exists in the first place. They need to align as a team on what's best for the program. This tool is the superglue that more senior program managers have handy to fill those cross-functional gaps.

### Influences without authority

Woven in tightly with the ability to rally consensus is the ability to influence without authority. You're the program manager and therefore the key facilitator and point of contact and you're viewed as a leader. You feel ownership for the success of the program and the program team who makes it happen, but no one reports to you. You have no authority to make anyone do anything. Instead, you need to have built the relationships and established the trust we spoke about above so that the team will listen to you. To do this, you will need to summon your leadership skills and self-confidence and sit down with that manager or C-level executive and remind them of the program goals and how you're depending on them to provide those resources needed for the work to be completed. You're not telling them what to do—you can't anyway! They don't have to do what you tell them. Rather you're influencing their thinking by reminding them why they need to get on board and do what's required for the program to be successful. I think this might be where my adjustable wrench comes in!

## Analytical

When I think about a program manager's analytical skills, the ability to break complex systems or problems down into meaningful parts, it's a saw that comes to mind. This tool is useful when a team is asked to develop a brand-new set of services and they can't figure out where to start. The program manager may propose a set of smaller incremental efforts along with a staggered delivery of the various services. They'll get the conversation started and usually it's not long before several potential solutions for how to proceed are on the table. The most talented program managers know how to use this tool with razor-like precision.

## Even-keeled temperament

In my family, I'm the cool cucumber, the one who is called upon when there's drama or something goes wrong. This skill has served me well as a program manager. Whatever the crisis, most people react emotionally and focus on the negative. The program manager is the one who calms everyone down and focuses on the solution and keeps everyone on the level (had to get that tool in somehow!). When I worked at Adobe, I managed a program manager with an MA in psychology who, in her previous career as a psychiatric social worker, had facilitated group therapy and family counseling sessions.

She was new to program management and commented to me that her background wouldn't be of any help. I smiled and assured her it would. Sure enough, a few months later she was facilitating a program team meeting and one of the managers lost his temper and stormed out of the room. Everyone was stunned and she instinctively jumped into action, calming everyone down and bringing the focus back to the purpose of the meeting to get things back on track. Whether you're a trained psychologist or have a computer science background, the ability to be the calm person in the room is essential to being a successful program manager.

## Supportive

When you support your program team members, they are able to achieve more than they could on their own. You have their back in tough situations and are a shoulder to cry on. And you are the first to congratulate them when they've achieved a milestone. This is your workbench, though I don't think it will fit in your tool belt!

## Good listener

What does it mean to be a good listener? It's not just about hearing what a team member is saying. It's about pausing, creating space, not interrupting when they hesitate, and listening deeply to what they're saying. It's about letting them speak and encouraging them to share. You're 100 percent focused on what they're saying. They're the most important person in the room. I liken this to a hole saw, you know, creating space?

### Empathetic

The best program managers are empathetic. They can tune in to a team member's emotions and will experience that same emotion. For example, they sense when a team member is struggling and automatically share in that struggle. They care about what their team member is dealing with and will do everything in their power to help them through it. Think of this as the first aid kit you keep handy in your workshop.

### Enjoys working behind the scenes

Finally, when I'm hiring a program manager, I always make sure that they enjoy working behind the scenes and are uninterested in the spotlight. They get their kicks from seeing things run smoothly due to good communication and planning. Okay, I'm all out of metaphors, but hopefully you've gotten the idea!

## Program Management Onboarding

When I started the Zendesk PMO, the onboarding included ten topics ranging from learning to use Confluence and understanding the company's annual goals to our program management methodology and the job ladder and job architecture.

I delivered this onboarding to a program manager who was brand-new to the role. I shudder to think how little I prepared her for the job. Just a few days into her tenure, I needed her to drive the completion of the development and launch of a brand-new cloud application. I'm happy to say that she managed to do that quite successfully and developed into an extremely talented program manager, despite our meager onboarding. Since those early (scary) pioneering days, the onboarding at Zendesk has developed into what is now a comprehensive program that takes several months to complete and assumes previous program management experience.

One of the benefits of a centralized PMO (p. 24) is having a set of program managers who are trained in a consistent methodology, who work in the same way across organizations. If you want this to happen across your company, the place to start is with onboarding. A program management onboarding program can and should be extensive to be effective. The one I designed for the Zendesk PMO takes months to complete. New hires from other reputable software companies told me it was much better than what they had at their previous companies—some said they didn't even receive any program management onboarding at all!

Building a top-notch PMO requires a well-thought-out and complete onboarding program that evolves over time to meet changing business needs. Here's a suggested outline for onboarding topics:

## Week One

☐ Attend the company's new hire orientation

☐ Complete basic workstation, hardware, and software set-up

☐ Learn about the products and services the company sells (p. 48)

☐ Meet your PMO buddy (p. 182)

In week one, the program manager starts learning about the programs they will drive forward and meets with PMO colleagues. This is a great time to assign a PMO buddy (p. 182) who can answer basic questions, such as where to find office supplies and where the best lunch places are. The new program manager should close out the week with some training on the products the company sells.

## Week Two

☐ Learn about PMO culture and best practices

    o  Mission, vision, values
    o  The company's annual planning process
    o  Setting up and running a program
    o  Status reporting (p. 78)

☐ Shadow a PMO colleague

☐ Attend a PMO welcome event

☐ Begin learning about the business for the organization you support

Week two usually has the program manager learning about the company's PMO culture and best practices. I like to allow time for the new hire to shadow several program managers, and if possible, I hold a PMO happy hour so that the program manager starts to feel like part of the team and knows they have the support of like-minded people. This is also a good place to get into business onboarding, which involves scheduling meet and greets with program/business teams and reviewing current and future priorities for the organization the program manager supports.

### Weeks Three and Four

☐ Set individual goals

☐ Take ownership of one or more programs

☐ Acquire additional knowledge

- ○ Issue and risk management best practices (p. 83)
- ○ Meeting management best practices (p. 123)
- ○ How the company's products and services are built
- ○ How to partner with your PMO colleagues on programs

Weeks three and four involve setting goals for the program manager, who begins to take ownership of the programs they will drive forward. This is a good time to learn some additional best practices, including issue and risk management, the software development lifecycle or other methodologies in use, meeting management, and how to partner with other program managers when your program is part of a portfolio of related programs.

### Week Five

☐ Begin driving programs with guidance

In week five, the program manager should be ready to put into practice what they've learned during weeks one through four.

Over the remainder of their first three months on the job, the program manager should continue their long-term education, which includes going deep on the organization(s) they support, learning about other related parts of the business, and presenting this knowledge to their manager and peers. (If you can explain it, you understand it.) Finally, I like to encourage each new program manager to find a domain in which to gain expertise, usually an area they're interested in and enthusiastic about, with the understanding that they may turn that into an onboarding session for the PMO one day. Some example areas of expertise might include risk management, change management, building stakeholder relationships, or creating a responsibility assignment matrix.

As your PMO practice evolves and the needs of the company change, I recommend you add new content to your onboarding, keep existing content updated, and retire any items no longer relevant on an ongoing basis. Either the program manager delivering the session should be responsible for keeping it updated or another subject matter expert in the PMO should own it. You might also consider assigning a senior member of the team the responsibility to review the onboarding content regularly, or perhaps a small group of interested program managers can ensure that it is meeting the needs of the team.

If a team member delivers an onboarding or reboarding (p. 191) session and feels that it's not up to date or up to par, I see it as their responsibility to either update it or contact the original author or their manager to get it updated. This is a team effort.

A comprehensive onboarding program is critical to developing a team of strong performers who program manage in a high-quality and consistent way. They'll be better equipped for their role, be more motivated, and feel loyal to the PMO and the company as a whole.

## Program Manager Buddies

You probably noticed that in week one of the onboarding process I suggested assigning a new PMO hire a program manager buddy. I've found that this sets up a new hire for success by helping them settle in, meet like-minded program managers, and feel like the PMO is their home away from home. Where possible, I assign a buddy who supports the same or a related organization and can therefore provide helpful context as needed.

Example pairings include two program managers supporting EMEA-based product development teams. The first time I did that at Zendesk, it went so well that when one of them buddied up with a newer program manager from our APAC region, the other wanted to know if they were still best buddies! In fact, all three still get along well and support one another several years later. If your company is global, you may end up needing to assign a buddy from a different office if the work done by the teams they support is spread across several locations. I prefer to err on the side of providing a buddy from the same geographic region, if possible, but as in the example above, they may be several time zones away. You can make this work with creative scheduling. For example, I've found that short daily check-ins for the first few weeks are helpful, and a longer weekly session allows for more in-depth conversations.

Not all pairings work perfectly but, in my experience, most endure. With an extensive onboarding program, a new program manager takes training sessions with several managers, so it's helpful to have a buddy at the same level as the new hire, so they feel comfortable to ask anything without fear of judgment. The buddy knows the lay of the land and usually knows some of the people on the team(s) the new program manager will be supporting. Sharing the inside scoop on what may or may not work with a particular person or team can save a newbie a lot of time.

I also recommend you document what the buddy program entails so that both program managers are clear on what's expected of them. That document should outline the reasons for the program, which might include relationship building, knowledge sharing, and employee retention. A buddy isn't a substitute for a manager nor are they expected to be a mentor. Their role is more about introducing the new program manager around, being available for questions, making sure the new hire is well integrated into the team and company, and providing that safe sounding board.

Consider including a checklist for the buddy in your documentation that describes what to do on day one (which includes lunch, if the two are in the same office), week one, month one, and the months thereafter. Typically, buddies remain paired for about six months but, as I said, the pairing often lingers, moving to a more informal relationship over the long term. If you want to start your own workplace buddy program, check out the Project Management Institute's 2014 article "Implementing a Buddy System in the Workplace" by John Cooper and Judy Wight.

## A Dual Job Ladder

In times past, the only way up the corporate ladder was to become a people manager, and that expression didn't even exist until about sixty years ago. The word "manager" was synonymous with "people manager." Today, many software companies have a dual ladder job structure that provides equivalent career opportunities for those who don't find people management satisfying and would prefer to continue in their role as an engineer, product manager, program manager, or financial analyst, for example. They can progress in their career as an individual contributor (IC) rather than as a people manager.

At all of the companies where I've worked as a program manager, a dual job ladder existed for program management. This means you can decide to become a people manager and work at it for several years. Then you can choose to become an IC again and make a lateral transition across the architecture, land at the same level, and then progress up the IC track.

When I started the PMO at Zendesk, I had to design the program management job ladder from scratch. I followed that with a companion job architecture where I outlined the job scope, required skills, responsibilities, expectations, and sphere of influence for the roles on both sides of the job ladder, whether managing people or programs. There are some overlapping skills on both sides of the job ladder and some that apply only to people managers. For example, for both people managers and for ICs, a high EQ (emotional quotient) level is required as well as experience as a program manager. That's because people managers in the PMO still drive programs, just not nearly as much as an IC whose role is strictly limited to managing programs.

People managers spend the majority of their time managing their direct reports and a limited amount of time driving programs forward. First-level people managers typically have a small team, perhaps two to three people, and are responsible for driving several programs. As they progress up the job ladder, usually they take on more people management and less day-to-day program management.

Managing a program or two keeps a program manager relevant and better able to understand the challenges faced by the people they manage. You stay up to date with tooling and processes, as well as the changing demands of the organizations that you and your team support. The programs you're driving will be more challenging than those of your direct reports. You have more experience, so it stands to reason that you should handle the trickier programs.

As the Zendesk PMO expanded from supporting just product development to supporting all organizations across the company and it organically became a centralized PMO (p. 24), I went from handling a program or two to only doing program management if someone was out of the office or we were short staffed. Once the headcount was secured again, I would step away as my day-to-day job was too demanding. As a substitute, I would occasionally sit in on program meetings and offer to review status reports (p. 78) so my program management skills wouldn't get rusty and I could still provide appropriate guidance as needed. I recommend this approach to PMO people managers if they don't have time to manage any programs.

I've seen several program managers go back and forth between people management and IC work to meet their work/life balance needs or their career interests. The flexibility in this model also allows PMO leadership to adjust their staff to meet business needs. Although encouraging someone to try a new skill set and watching them grow and develop is satisfying for a manager as well as the individual, it also provides some give and take in staffing that a high-growth business requires. The trick is in making the right moves with the right people at the right time!

One final note: the levels you create on your job ladder must map to the standard Radford job codes, or whatever global job-leveling framework is used by your company. This provides consistency with roles outside of your company when your program managers are representing themselves in their external network.

## Learning Is a Constant

Developing our employees is the most important thing we do as people managers, so we should take it seriously. You can foster continuous development by presenting training on relevant and timely topics at team meetings and offsites to keep the skills of your program management team fresh. The last stage of the onboarding process discussed earlier (p. 177) has the new program manager learning the business of their teams and the company, as well as finding and developing an area of interest they can specialize in and share with the rest of the PMO. When you're working for a fast-growing company, you remain relevant by continuing to evolve how you work. Enter continuing education.

Many companies have an annual planning process that includes an update to the long-range plan as well as the plan for the coming year. Teams are asked to create their annual plans and the PMO is no exception. Program managers should always be on the lookout for opportunities to expand their skill set and evolve their methodology and best practices. Building employee development into your team's annual plan is one way to ensure it happens. Continuing education can take place in many different ways, but here are some suggestions that I've found to be creative and helpful.

### Add onboarding sessions

Consider adding onboarding sessions as your company evolves, so that you're serving the business in the best way possible. Sessions might focus on becoming a trusted partner, tools for working across geographies, strategies for more effectively working from home, handling mid-quarter pop-up requests, working more strategically, or learning to delegate.

### Introduce program spotlights

In a fast-growing company, new products and services are continuously added. Program spotlights on these additions are a great way to inform the broader PMO of things that are likely to impact most, if not all, organizations at the company. An example might be the company's need to support a new regulation such as the EU's General Data Protection Regulation (GDPR).

### Evolve best practices

Reviewing and updating best practices keeps a program manager on top of things, especially where nurturing relationships is concerned. One of the Zendesk program managers shared with the PMO his walk and talk process to build stakeholder relationships and keep abreast of potential changes, which allowed him to better mitigate risk. It involved a forty-five-minute walk around beautiful Copenhagen, and maybe a cup of coffee.

## Collaborate on change

Changes to process should be regularly shared. The product development and marketing program managers at Zendesk collaborated on an improved pre-launch checklist and shared that with the PMO, since building and launching software products is what companies like Zendesk do. At Adobe, a new process for presenting new product ideas to management for approval was shared with program managers at an optional lunch and learn. These kinds of sessions could be added to an onboarding curriculum, as appropriate.

## Take advantage of training

Many companies provide an annual professional development budget for employees. Program managers can take advantage of this benefit in a big way with training in areas such as group facilitation skills, positive psychology and leadership, multi-stakeholder collaboration, and speaking in front of small and large audiences. Technical program managers might find courses on agile and Scrum methodologies useful. Some companies allow that budget to be used to hire a mentor or coach for development specific to an individual employee's needs.

## See you at the improv

One Zendesk program manager participates in an improvisation course as a hobby. She invited me to see her perform when I visited her office in France. When she came to our headquarters in San Francisco, I suggested she put the program managers through an improv training session. She was perplexed at first, wondering how that could possibly be useful. I reminded her how often in her job she was required to think on her feet. "Oui, okay, I'll do it!" she agreed. The session was a resounding success. She spent an hour with the program managers, taking everyone through a variety of exercises that required them to think and act on their feet. Everyone found it helpful, relevant, and a lot of fun!

## The Spice of Life

Program managers are generally assigned to an organization and stick with it for quite a while. But giving a program manager something different to work on has advantages for them as well as for the business.

Program managers are a funny bunch (I can say that because I'm one of them). We are usually Type A people who like to be busy. As any good people manager does, I check in regularly with my direct reports to make sure their workload, and that of their teams, is manageable. I've gotten the request more than once to "work on something different." They're plenty busy, they love the teams they support, they just want some variety in their work.

You'll find that as your PMO grows and continues to add value, you'll receive requests for additional program management support. I like to find a way to accommodate these requests if they're suitable for my team. Often the request doesn't come with headcount, but if the work is important for the company, or for the community in which the company is located, I'm always motivated to find a match.

One such request came from the Zendesk CEO who had been spearheading the development of the alley behind the company headquarters to make it safer and less attractive to the drug dealers who were frequenting it. The Zendesk social impact team joined city leaders to support improvements that included increased lighting, repaving the street, a basketball court, food trucks, and painted murals. That team needed help pulling the program together and driving it forward. The cross-functional aspect required some of the usual internal connecting of dots but also involved communicating with city government offices, which was something new for the program manager I suggested for the effort. "Was she interested?," I asked. "Sign me up!" Not only did it provide some variety from her daily work supporting a product development team, it gave her insight into community efforts, and she got some exposure to our CEO. All in all, it was a wonderful learning experience for her and met her need for something different to work on.

At a large company like Adobe, there are a variety of product and service teams, which makes it easy for a program manager to get experience in other areas of the business. One program manager volunteered to help establish an executive shadowing program for women. She not only lent her valuable skills to the effort but also did something good for an underrepresented group at the company while making lasting connections with employees across the business.

At Macromedia, a lead program manager recognized that the product packaging (back in the days when software products were delivered to customers on disks with printed documentation) could be made less expensive. She worked with the appropriate business leads to define goals for reducing costs and worked cross-functionally to assemble a team and drive it forward. She learned a lot in the process and directly impacted the company's bottom line. If you're creative and motivated, the opportunities for learning are endless.

Repurposing program managers across organizations takes some planning and requires patience on the part of the requesting organization, as some time may be required to get a program manager up to speed. But the effort certainly meets the goal of adding variety to the program manager's work and gives PMO leadership some flexibility in allocating resources across the company—a win-win situation.

## Reboarding

Developing your employees is one of the most important things a PMO leader does, and it's important to make sure that no balls are dropped during an employee's onboarding. If a ball does get dropped, let the employee know you're going to make sure they get onboarded appropriately to whatever topic they missed out on. I've also found that a program manager might want to sit through an onboarding session again to refresh their knowledge. I like to call this activity reboarding. Reboarding might be needed when:

- The employee realizes they didn't quite "grok" the topic and wants to take the onboarding session again.

- The employee took the session early in their tenure before they had on-the-job experience and it wasn't relevant at the time.

- The onboarding session has changed extensively since they attended and they would like a refresher.

- Their manager sees a gap in their performance and suggests the employee sit through the onboarding session again.

Whatever the reason, reboarding should be done in a timely manner. Depending on the situation, you have the following options:

- **Involuntary reboarding:** If the reboarding is involuntary, you'll need to have a conversation with the employee about what you or a team member or stakeholder has observed, and then suggest a refresh on the topic. This is usually done individually, with a focus on the areas you think are the most important.

- **Voluntary reboarding:** This is usually done as a group session where you present the topic to the employee in question and to anyone else who wants to join in.

If you think your employee isn't open to reboarding, you could suggest they read Carol Dweck's book *Mindset: The New Psychology of Success* (and make sure you've read it as well). This book can help someone understand that if they have a growth mindset, they are more likely to learn and therefore be more successful in their career. Employees have told me it flipped a switch for them, and I've watched them go from zero to sixty in their learning and progression.

## Key Takeaways

- As program managers develop, they should build an impressive set of skills or superpowers to handle just about any situation that comes their way.

- Develop a robust onboarding curriculum to ensure your program management practice is top-notch and consistent across the business.

- A dual job ladder provides upward mobility for program managers who have no interest in or aptitude for people management.

- A program manager buddy assigned to a newly hired program manager offers them a safe place to ask basic questions and helps them integrate.

- Learning is a constant. Consider presenting topics at your PMO all hands meeting and then add those topics to the onboarding if appropriate to keep it up to date.

- Program managers like variety in their work. Help them look for opportunities outside of the teams they officially support so they can broaden their knowledge of the business or their community and apply their skills with greater impact.

- Reboarding a program manager on a topic is a great option if they're struggling in a particular area, or if the content has changed.

# 10

# MAKING
# THE GRADE

By now you understand what to look for in good program manager candidates and how to get them onboarded. Helping your program managers make the grade is what this section is all about. It's the advanced course in program management so the people in the organization you support will see you as a strategic thinker, a trusted partner for advice, and the one person they can rely on to make things right in their teams. You won't have to ask to be invited to the party anymore—your seat is reserved in advance!

Master these skills and you'll have made the grade:

☐ Think and work more strategically

☐ Keep your objectivity intact

☐ Learn to influence without authority

☐ Become a trusted advisor

☐ Get comfortable with ambiguity

☐ Own responsibility for the end-to-end program

☐ Be on the lookout for opportunities to add value

☐ Be aware of your perfectionist tendencies

☐ Use your skills to give back

## What It Means to Be Strategic

If you haven't figured it out by now, I espouse the type of program management know as strategic program management: program managers drive forward complex cross-functional programs that map to and move the needle on the company strategy. This requires that a program manager be strategic, and that requirement increases as they progress up the career ladder. Over the years, I've had several program managers ask me to explain what it means to be strategic, so let me unpack my thoughts on this.

Understanding the broader context in which you work and zooming in and out as you drive a program forward are key to being a successful program manager. At kickoff, it's important that the team members are clear on why the program exists. These are the questions the program manager and the program team should be able to answer to ensure the team's work is focused on company priorities and moves the needle on the company strategy:

• What's the company goal that the program ladders up to?

• What problem are you trying to solve?

- How does the program accomplish that?

- What things need to happen to execute on this strategic priority effectively?

- What internal and external forces might have a positive or negative impact on this program?

Now that you have your priorities straight, and the team is off and running, as program manager you should be driving the train down the track, keeping the team focused on the next few milestones, and keeping an eye on potential risks that might need mitigating so the program stays on schedule. This requires a focus on details: When is that next milestone due? What has to happen exactly for successful completion of that part of the program? Who needs to be involved?

But while that's going on, you need to stay abreast of the strategic context in which you are operating. The questions below are the kinds of things a strategic program manager should be thinking about during the lifecycle of a program:

- Have changes been made to the company strategy that impact the organization you support? Does that change the work being done for this program?

- Are there technology considerations that might necessitate changes to the program?

- Are the economics of the industry impacted in such a way that changes to your program may be needed?

- Has a competitor done something that requires the team to reconsider the scope or timeline for the program?

- Is there another external situation (a worldwide pandemic, for example) that requires a change in strategy? How will that impact the portfolio of programs already underway?

Good program managers are proactive about making sure that when the train comes barreling through the next few stops, nothing is in the way. In a strategic context, this means being aware of everything both internally and externally around the program you are driving. It means knowing what your PMO colleagues are working on and how those efforts might be interdependent or impact your program. You should be on the lookout for opportunities to share work or gain efficiencies, and be open to innovations that would speed up the work for your program and other related programs, all in service of the company strategy.

In the first few years of their careers, program managers usually have some ability to be strategic. They learn how to zoom in to the program details and zoom out to the broader strategic context but only occasionally. As the person advances in their program management career, they can adjust their lens more frequently. More senior program managers and those on the PMO leadership team know how to zoom in and out every day, and often several times in one meeting. That ability to focus on both the macro and the micro develops with experience and the right kind of guidance.

If you're just getting started as a program manager, you can develop your strategic thinking. Here are some ideas to get you started:

- Make sure you understand the company goals and can explain them to a PMO peer.

- Get to know the business for the organization you support.

- Make sure you can articulate the key priorities for the organization you support and how those priorities move the needle on the company strategy.

- Learn about the businesses you are dependent on. One way to do this is to have other program managers explain how the organization they support functions. The marketing program manager, for example, can explain how a product gets launched. Follow up by inviting that program manager for coffee to discuss the details of your interdependent programs.

The more you understand the world around you, the better able you are to spot trends, problems, and opportunities that will impact the program(s) you are driving. Your business leads will see your value not only as a facilitator who drives the program forward but as a strategic partner who truly understands their business and its context. And I guarantee you'll have more positive impact and find greater job satisfaction.

## No Taking Sides

Researchers spend a lot of time observing their subjects. If they're not careful, they can become so involved with and sympathetic to the group that they lose objectivity. An extreme example of this general principle is Stockholm syndrome, when hostages begin to sympathize with their captors even at gunpoint and may adopt, at least temporarily, their ideological views. Though a program manager can't be taken hostage by the team they support, it is crucial that when conflicts arise, they remain objective and consider the needs of the program over any team drama or politics.

Program managers become aware of conflicts or potential conflicts by understanding what motivates each team member and stakeholder. They are ready when the product manager says that the engineering work must be sped up to meet the desired release date, and when the engineering lead responds that it's impossible to meet that deadline. In this scenario, it's the job of the program manager to remain objective and get the team aligned. Program managers may have an opinion, but they must bury their opinions and focus on what's right for the program.

Good program managers spend a significant amount of time with the team members they support. Often, they are colocated with them, in an embedded fashion. The program manager often sees themselves as part of the team or organization they are supporting. They build relationships and even make friends with team members, which is half the fun of being part of a team. The organization begins to believe that the program manager is on *their* team. That's a good thing, right? Well, only partly. The challenge is that program managers need to remain objective so that *all* team members know they can turn to the program manager if a conflict arises.

If a program manager is too well integrated, they lose their objectivity. You will hear this change when they speak of "my team" or "we" when referring to the team they support. And you will hear them express an opinion in favor of one team member over another, or will favor their team over a dependent team in another organization. This change in objectivity often shows up when the program manager moves from occasionally sitting with or near the team they support to always sitting with them.

The point is that the program manager is now lobbying for particular people, and that means they are lobbying against some others. When team members see a program manager taking sides, they lose trust in their ability to be objective. So how do you fix this?

One way I've handled this it to have the program manager sit for half the week with the team they are supporting and the other half with other program managers. Results are usually immediate, and the program managers always thank me for extracting them from a situation they didn't even realize they were in. By all means, spend time with the team you're supporting to build relationships and stay in the loop—that's a requirement. Just make sure you aren't spending all your time with them and playing favorites. Remember, the ultimate goal is a successful program, and that requires objectivity.

Some program managers get this concept right away and never need this kind of intervention. Immediately upon starting his new role at Zendesk, a seasoned program manager shared his time between his PMO colleagues in a neighboring building and the team he supports. Masterfully done!

But once in a while, someone will say to me, "Gosh, I wish our program manager would share their opinion now and then." I get it. Your program manager is knowledgeable, and you'd like them to weigh in. However, the good ones know how to share the options on the table and prompt discussion on the pros and cons of each. They remind everyone of the program goals and what's best for its success. And they facilitate to get alignment. In my world, this always works best when it's done without taking sides.

# Objectivity builds trust.

## Influencing without Authority

"Program managers have all of the responsibility for a program's success but no actual authority to make it happen." If you're a program manager, you've definitely heard this one. This comment is the bane of our existence! But just how do you get people who don't report to you to do what you're asking?

I worked closely with a business lead in Finance who coined the term "pleasantly persistent" when referring to a program manager he worked closely with and trusted implicitly. On several occasions throughout a particularly trying program (aren't they all!), she had to ask him and his team to do things they didn't want to do or that were messy to do. But she managed to convince them. Each time she approached them, they'd see her coming down the aisle and they'd smile and pretend to run the other way. In the end, they were great about stepping up and doing what was required to move the program forward. So how did she get there?

If I could choose one thing for a program manager to focus on, it's building relationships with program team members and those on dependent teams. Start with the executive sponsor for your program. Set up some time to chat so you can understand what they're trying to accomplish. Align with them on how this program moves the needle on the company strategy. Ask them what they're most excited about and what keeps them up at night. Do this over coffee if you can, so that you get to know them as a person. Open with a personal question or two. For example, you heard they grew up in Paris, or they love to go kiteboarding, or they were a high school chess champion. Share something about yourself but don't go on too long; this is about you getting to know them.

Usually it's a wonderful thing to be part of a team. You're all working toward a common goal, sharing in the ups and downs. You're getting to know each other as colleagues and team members and as people. So what happens when you need one of those team members to change direction, to do something you're pretty sure they're not going to want to do? You start with the why.

Lead with why what you are about to ask them to do or change is important. Don't wait until the end of the pitch. If you want your request to have a chance, and you've built a good rapport with the person in the first place, an explanation of why the request for the change is important, followed by friendly prodding, will be effective. People must be willing to listen to you before they even consider agreeing to do what you are asking, and still want to have lunch with you afterward.

Remember they don't report to you and they don't have to listen to you. Technically they don't have to do a single thing you ask, but they usually will if you've established a rapport. You like and trust each other. You stay calm even when they don't and help them see reason. You don't raise your voice, push them around, or insist they do what you're asking. That tactic is guaranteed to fail and make matters worse if they are already upset.

You definitely don't want to be seen as a nag, so you'll need to disarm them to bring them around—this may require that you first fall on your sword, whether the change needed is your fault or not. Then remind them why the thing you're asking them to do is important for the success of the program and the company. As the person calms down, ask for their collaboration. When a program manager is good at this kind of diplomacy, eventually the person will understand what has to be done. It may take several days or even weeks, so be patient. Even if they don't totally agree, they'll get on board and do what's being asked of them. And when they do, make sure to thank them appropriately, in front of the program team, in an email with their manager cc'd, or with a nice bottle of their favorite wine. Or all three!

## You Are a Trusted Advisor

Strategic program managers execute on company strategy. They partner closely with their business lead to execute on the goals that lead has to move that strategy forward. That business lead may be a first-level manager, a mid-level manager, or a company executive. In all cases, the program manager can become a trusted advisor to their business partner. This levels up their participation from simple execution to a role where the business partner uses them as a sounding board and seeks out their advice. This benefit to the business partner means the program manager's impact to the program and organization is that much greater. And that feels good. So how do you become that trusted advisor?

### Learn the business

First you need to learn everything about the organization's business, be it finance, IT, security, or marketing.

- Listen deeply and learn about what your business leader wants to accomplish.

- Study the business and read whatever supporting documentation is available.

- Ask your business partners to describe what they're trying to accomplish. You can even ask them to draw a picture on a whiteboard.

- Learn what success looks like to them and understand what has them worried. (This will also help you fill out your risk register.)

- Ask those same questions of business leaders at all levels of the organization you support.

The more you know about the business, the better a program manager you will be. You'll be able to follow the discussions in meetings, offer suggestions, steer the conversation as needed to keep the team focused on the program goal(s), and mitigate risks.

### Use your 1:1 meeting time wisely

When you have a 1:1 meeting with your business lead, it's imperative to use the time well. This is the time to update them on the status of the program and any pending risks or issues they need a heads-up on before going into a meeting with a key stakeholder or executive staff. This is also a great time to shine a light on other things they may not be aware of. But you'll need to understand how much detail your business lead wants. Some will find the details too low level and others won't be comfortable without them. This meeting time coupled with your keen understanding of the business will kickstart that trust process.

### Be a sounding board

When your business lead is treating you as a true partner and confidante, they start to show their cards, sharing their frustrations and concerns. They feel they can let down their hair with you and vent a bit. They're trusting you so remember that anything they share in confidence must be kept under wraps for that trust to be preserved. Listen, nod, be empathetic, and as they wrap up the vent session, be encouraging about how you will all get past whatever situation appears daunting.

But what about the second word in the phrase "trusted advisor"? You've arrived as a program manager when the business leader or executive asks for your advice. Draw on your business knowledge and everything you know about the program, the key players, and the strategic context to suggest a way forward. But avoid going on a long diatribe about everything that's wrong with the program. Instead, ask questions to draw them out, share a suggestion, and then rinse and repeat throughout the lifecycle of the program. You'll be helping them more than ever before, and this part of your job may well have the most impact. Game on!

## Getting Comfortable with Ambiguity

In today's dynamic world, ambiguity is baked into the work you're doing, which adds complexity and makes decisions more difficult. Those who can deal with ambiguity and even get comfortable with it will be more successful.

What does ambiguity look like for a program? Sometimes it's a lack of direction from the top: it may not be clear what management is asking the team to do, or an executive sponsor might not be specific about intentions. You almost never have all the answers before starting up a program. In fact, you may only know the end goal and have a vague idea about how to go about reaching it. And that's okay! As program manager, you kick off the program and present its goals to get alignment from program team members. You present what's known and what's still to be answered. You're the one who talks about the need for agility as the team moves forward, since time is money and competitors aren't waiting. You will get clarification eventually, but ambiguity won't paralyze you and the team in the meantime. Program managers who are comfortable with ambiguity can move forward despite not having all of the answers.

Here's how do that:

- Proceed calmly and pragmatically; program work needs to move forward despite any ambiguity.

- Create two lists in your mind: the known quantities and the open questions.

- Think through next steps for filling in the blanks:

    o Who do you need to sit down with to dig into a particular open question?

    o Who should be invited to the program meeting to share their domain expertise?

    o What other information is available that might provide answers?

You will work hard to ensure information and answers are gathered as the program progresses, in a timely manner, to keep things moving forward. Draw on the expertise of the people around you, since their knowledge is different from your own, and encourage them to offer up their ideas as you all move toward clarity. Encouraging the team to take some calculated risks when not everything is known is usually a solid strategy for the program manager—often it's your only strategy! You need the ability to keep the train moving even as track ahead is still being laid (p. 68). It can be done.

I can tell when someone is struggling with ambiguity. They pepper the room with a million questions, most of which they know can't be answered. They are so focused on frantically getting answers that they don't stop to realize they're the only one in the room asking questions, that everyone else is okay with the ambiguity. Those people need to be taken aside and gently made to understand that they need to get with the program, so to speak! It's the program manager's job to inject calm into these individuals and create confidence in the team's ability to work with ambiguity.

As program manager, it's also important to understand your own tolerance level for ambiguity, and then work to raise it. If you're struggling to function when the work isn't completely clear, it might be a good idea to seek out your manager or a mentor who can help you with some of the strategies mentioned above to move forward regardless and adapt as you go. Comfort with ambiguity is the key to success.

## Owning the Whole Food Chain

One of my product development program managers at Zendesk drove a complex program that took about a year and a half from start to finish. It involved moving customer data from one environment to another. She was familiar with the technical gory details that it took to make this happen, but she also got to know the stakeholders along the whole food chain, including the very end of that chain, namely the manager on the customer success team responsible for notifying customers that their data was going to be moved. The customer success manager had to explain to the end customer why the move was needed, choose an appropriate date for the move, and do some amount of prep work on the data to ensure a smooth transition.

Later, that program manager traveled from her office to the headquarters in San Francisco for a periodic check-in. The customer success manager crossed paths with her in a meeting and literally jumped for joy at seeing her and gave her a big hug. That customer success manager was so happy with the partnership, and it was a sign to me that the program manager truly understood what it meant to own the deliverable from end to end. It's a fantastic example of a solid relationship that a program manager can have with their key stakeholders, and it warms my heart when I get to see it play out.

I define the role of program manager as strategic execution: driving end-to-end cross-functional initiatives that move broader complex goals forward. When I say "end to end," I mean it. A program manager who supports the product development team is responsible not only for getting the product or feature designed, developed, tested, and deployed but also for ensuring the marketing team is ready to launch it, sales is enabled to sell it, customer success can ensure a happy customer, and so on.

To do this efficiently, consider using pair program management (p. 117). The program manager at the source of the deliverable is the single point of contact but partners closely with one or more additional program managers from the stakeholder teams to ensure everything from end to end goes as planned. For example, the product development program manager meets regularly with the marketing, sales, and customer success program managers to sync on upcoming milestones and to discuss issues that may impact timelines, interdependencies, and risks.

The program manager plays an important role in ensuring the program team is accountable for the success of the end-to-end program rather than just the piece they are on the hook to contribute. That would be considered "throwing it over the wall" and hoping everything else goes to plan. That doesn't fly with me. A program manager's job isn't done until a sales representative is able to talk to customers about the product and get a signature and hear back from the customer that they're happy. Perfect.

## Yin and Yang: Program Managers and Creatives

Sometimes the opportunity to add value arises where you might not have expected your skills to be welcome or useful, where the work is so different that it may not seem obvious how program management can help. It's important to be on the lookout for such opportunities, and you may not even know how to help until you peel back the layers and get involved. The story below is one such example.

Creative types and program managers engage in different work, yet their roles are complementary. Like the interplay between yin and yang, each plays an important role in the development of software to form a dynamic system in which the whole is greater than the sum of its parts. I had first-hand experience of this when I collaborated closely with the Zendesk brand team. Given that my background is in software engineering, at our first few meetings I felt like a super geek surrounded by a bunch of good-looking, artistic, well-dressed movie stars. It wasn't hard to visualize myself as Mr. Spock on the deck of the Starship *Enterprise*: a Vulcan among humans.

Our first task together was on a more effective quarterly planning process for the brand team. As a services team that spends a lot of their cycles supporting the marketing team, the brand team had been unable to make adequate time to move the needle on the Zendesk brand. They felt powerless and were resigned to "never being able to work on the cool things." That's when I entered the mix.

I modified their usual planning process by first asking Zendesk's chief creative officer, Toke Nygaard, for his top-down priorities: his vision of where he wanted the team to go. The team chimed in as well, elaborating on these priorities and surfacing a few additional ideas. By creating programs centered on these priorities, we made it possible to carve out more time for brand-driven priorities in just a couple of quarters. Together we committed to move that work forward alongside the required deliverables for marketing, and to hold the brand team accountable with weekly check-ins and clear success measures. After this modified process was implemented and positive results were visible, one of the brand team leaders remarked, "Hey, this planning stuff really works!" Yes, it does.

This rejiggering of priorities and focus on moving the needle on the brand allowed the team to spend almost a year digging into a key initiative around Zendesk brand quality and consistency. With a newly hired brand program manager, the goals and objectives for this initiative surfaced quickly, and we strategized on the best way to get this program off the ground. That began with weekly program team meetings (p. 77).

As I listened to the various creative leads describe what they wanted to accomplish, I hesitantly suggested that a prioritization framework might help move the work forward. The room went quiet and suddenly I felt like a redshirt about to get a lethal phaser blast, but after that awkward pause came an "Awesome!" That was when I truly began to see the value of complementary skill sets to move a program forward, to bring a key initiative to life. The team continued to make good progress on this initiative, piloting several very successful brand projects as part of the broader program and increasing stakeholder engagement across the company. And they're super encouraged by what they've accomplished and how they were able to level up the team's impact across the company.

This is a great example of how the combination of creatives and program managers is an effective one. I learned a lot more about the positive impact of these complementary skill sets applied to a program, it was a lot of fun, and, as a side effect, I learned to dress better. The whole is definitely greater than the sum of its parts!

## Program Managers Don't Have B Games

The skills required to do the job of program manager effectively mean that person is a high achiever who demands nothing less than perfection from themselves to ensure a well-run program. That's great as long as you can dial back those tendencies with your program team members. It's also important to maintain a good work/life balance for longevity in your career.

When the PMO was in its infancy at Zendesk, and as the first program was launching, the executive sponsor, my esteemed former colleague Sam Boonin, came into the room as we were rolling things out live to customers. The rollout was well planned in advance, and dry runs were held until we were sure we were ready to go. On game day, we were executing the rollout and he was a little surprised that things were so calm and quiet. He looked around the room and said, "This is what good looks like." Yes it is.

In Chapter Nine, I talked about the superpowers that program managers must wield to do a great job. That pretty much makes them superheroes, and I think that's an accurate assessment. Program managers tend to have type A personalities; they're high achievers and get their kicks from seeing things run smoothly. They also have some quirks: I've had program managers express their dissatisfaction in their performance just as I'm giving them a raise, or be surprised and list several reasons why they're not sure they deserve it. I once described a potential solution as "adequate" and got wrinkled noses from the program managers around the table. It has to be great, excellent, or, well, perfect in order for them to feel satisfied.

Sometimes I find myself suggesting that a program manager "dial it back ever so slightly" (and then I duck for my own safety!). I do get concerned about their stress levels and remind them that most mere mortals operate on a different plane. They need to slightly lower the high expectations they hold for themselves when dealing with their cross-functional team members. Once when I was at a Zendesk meeting with all the program managers assembled, we were discussing how to manage our stress levels, given our company's high-growth environment. One program manager asked for suggestions on how to dial back their A game and another replied matter-of-factly, "I don't have a B game." We all laughed but acknowledged the need to strike a balance between ensuring a program goes off without a hitch and burning out.

I'm happy to say that program managers across the industry are generally a very collaborative bunch. They quite readily reach out to their PMO colleagues who are always at the ready with advice and assistance. I saw this at Adobe, where the company is so large that the PMO is no longer centralized, but the collaboration among program managers across vast and varied functions continues. That team spirit serves to remind them that they all face similar challenges. Armed with an effective methodology and their A games (tempered as needed), these highly skilled professionals will and do get their programs successfully across the line.

## Time to Give Back

To wrap up this chapter on "Making the Grade," let's look for opportunities to use those program manager superpowers for the greater good. Here are a few ideas and stories that may inspire you to get out there and share your talents.

## Mentoring

Effective mentoring is something I've always been passionate about. In the early days of my career, I began nurturing a set of mentors without fully realizing the benefits of my efforts, but I absolutely understood the value of their feedback. As I progressed in my career, I was sought out as a mentor. Now I mentor many people and continue to seek advice from my own mentors. After all, we are all works in progress and my growth mindset will, I hope, always be a part of my life. One of my mentors is good at challenging my assumptions, which helps me to get to the heart of the matter.

Mentoring is a key part of my professional life in technology. For example, when I was leading the PMO at Zendesk, I was inspired to assist the diversity and inclusion (D&I) department in creating a mentoring program after the CFO, Elena Gomez, gathered all the female senior leaders together to address the key issues facing women at Zendesk. D&I is a very relevant topic, and although diversity in hiring is important, we all felt strongly that retention must be a companion focus area. So we set about to create a women's mentoring program.

The D&I team signed up to design the framework and develop the content and asked for program management help to pull the effort together into a program and drive it from start to finish. I was happy to help, along with one of my technical program managers supporting the product development team. Her involvement was a game changer as she had established solid relationships in product management, product design, and engineering and was able to recruit a product manager, a designer, several developers, a test engineer, and a database administrator to join the effort. Partnering with D&I as the subject matter experts, she formed a team that designed, built, tested, and deployed a pilot web application. I served as executive sponsor. We planned to mentor about twenty-five women. We announced the pilot globally and ended up with 140 women seeking mentorship. So I shoulder-tapped about fifty more mentors, and the pilot was successfully completed with much positive feedback. We learned a great deal and from there the Zendesk D&I team took it forward.

Without a program manager to keep us all motivated and on schedule despite the fact that the program was not a top priority from a business perspective, this pilot would not have been so successful. We all took great satisfaction in knowing we provided mentoring as well as networking opportunities for 140 women across the company.

There was no budget for a large team to do this work, let alone a full-time program manager, so stepping up to help was a worthwhile cause. It's important to note that the team designing and developing the mentoring app was also comprised of volunteers. They were primarily women, but we had some support from a few men in engineering as well. The program manager was able to rally that support by tapping into her well-developed network of team members and stakeholders. And a little cajoling didn't hurt!

Program managers enjoy having a program or two to drive that are a bit out of their main focus area to provide them with some variety and, in this case, with the knowledge that they're doing good work too. This is a prime example of how putting in that extra effort and applying our program management superpowers can make the world a better place.

### Sharing your skills with nonprofits

The culture at Zendesk is such that employees are pretty involved in the neighborhoods where they're based. The company has an active social impact program, and executive leadership enthusiastically encourages and supports employee participation in that program. Zendesk commits six hours of volunteering per employee per year, at over 100 nonprofits around the globe, through its #6 HourPledge.

When it was the PMO's turn to give back, we were inspired by the Zendesk marketing team, who had volunteered with local nonprofits by imparting marketing skills they could use going forward. So the program managers decided we would do something similar.

Few nonprofits have trained program managers who can develop and drive programs for their organizations. That's where the Zendesk PMO, a team of professional program managers who are darn good at what they do, stepped in. We worked with the social impact team to determine if nonprofits might be interested in some program management training, and the answer was a resounding "yes!" Volunteers from within the PMO stepped up, and the resulting team, led by a senior team member, developed a two-hour training class to teach basic skills such as:

- Goal setting and prioritization
- Building and using a schedule
- Stakeholder management
- Schedule management
- Cost management
- Issue and risk management
- Status reporting

The PMO team held training sessions in nine global locations, with twenty-four nonprofit organizations participating, and a total of fifty-two employees at those nonprofits attending. The feedback was extremely positive, with 100 percent of participants saying the training would help them succeed in their job. Over thirty program managers from around the globe participated and donated 144 hours of their time. But it wasn't just the nonprofit attendees who felt positive afterward. The program managers who participated said they felt good about the work they did, with one saying, "It was great to be able to leverage my skill set to immediately add value to these organizations. I felt that this session will reach many more people than a one-time volunteer event would." Another said, "We have the chance to make a positive impact on the programs that our Zendesk Neighborhood Foundation partners are working on." And yet another program manager remarked about teaming up with other program managers for the effort that "it's great to understand how others manage their programs and learn from them."

As with any effort, the business team—in this case, the small but mighty Zendesk social impact team with the subject matter expertise in working with nonprofits—partnered closely with the PMO to pave the way for this wonderful training. It was a new and different idea, and they were all over it! One of the goals of the social impact team is to "improve the efficiency and impact of a global set of nonprofits that provide neighborhood services by donating Zendesk software and expertise." I can safely say that with the help and expertise of the social impact team, these wonderful program management volunteers did just that—and came away feeling invigorated. Not bad for several afternoons of work!

Congratulations, program managers! You've now learned the secrets to making the grade as a program manager. I encourage you to stay committed to developing your skill set and if you are a people manager to pass on those skills to the next generation of talented program managers. Continue to make the role of program manager one of positive impact and add value to your teams and the company where you work, and keep those trains running smoothly!

# CONCLUSION

W ell, my train is pulling into its final station stop. If you are a company owner/operator and looking to add program management to your business, I've shared with you my recommendations on how to build and run a PMO in your company. And if you are a program manager, you now know the secrets to my success and how to level up your skills. It's your turn to put on the conductor's cap.

My wealth of experience in this field has enabled me to demonstrate and pass on how program management makes a valuable impact on teams and companies. As the world becomes increasingly connected, and the competitive landscape more intense, the work is ever more complex and companies struggle to keep up. Everyone needs to find ways to perform more efficiently and effectively to bring their strategic vision to life.

Program management plays a critical role in bringing people together, across functional and geographic boundaries, to help companies achieve their strategic goals. And although program management is a relatively new discipline, more and more companies are adopting it.

The program managers I've trained and managed have had a front row seat to my passion for this discipline. I personally mentor many program managers across several industries, and I wrote this book to share with them and all of you what I've learned over the years about how to make program management a more formalized and respected discipline alongside the likes of engineering, product management, and product marketing.

And as more companies adopt program management, they'll wrestle with many of the topics I've surfaced in this book: about how to structure their PMO, socialize it, fund it, and recruit and develop program managers so that their work has a positive impact and their PMO adds value to the company, giving them an edge over their competitors.

The enthusiastic response to my writing on social media is evidence of the desire across a variety of industries to learn more about this discipline and bring it to the forefront. To that end, I'll continue to promote program management and the ongoing development of program managers everywhere via those channels and through my mentoring and my profession.

# ACKNOWLEDGMENTS

—○—

I begin by thanking Adrian McDermott, who took a chance on me and let me build the Zendesk PMO from the ground up. You challenged me at all the right times and then got out of my way. Your trust and support meant so much.

To Morten Primdahl for his genuine interest during my journey building the Zendesk PMO and his forethought in encouraging me to write down my story.

Dushka Zapata, you are a gem! Your advice in those early days about how to approach this project and revel in the writing process was invaluable.

Thanks to everyone at Page Two Books for taking on this project. Special thanks to Trena White and Amanda Lewis for shepherding me through the process, and a shout-out to master editor Sarah Brohman, whose expert hand gave structure to my story. I couldn't have done it without you.

I'm grateful to Karen Catlin, a program management pioneer and colleague at Go, Macromedia, and Adobe, who pointed me to Page Two and whose own writing and publishing journey gave me the courage to write this book.

To everyone in the Zendesk PMO and Operations teams, who are the most talented, hardworking, and wonderful colleagues I've ever had. You showed up every day and gave your best, and then some, and patiently put up with my high bar and strong opinions about our "craft." All of you will always hold a special place in my heart.

Writing this book was a labor of love. I think about my sister, Mary, who left us much too soon and never got to finish her first book. My father, Arthur, managed to write and publish four books in his retirement. His lifelong passion for learning and teaching, and his towering intellect remain with me as a constant reminder of how to live a life of purpose and give back to so many until "we go poof." Thanks, Dad!

Finally, to my husband, Michael, my greatest cheerleader, for his unwavering support and love as I spent many weeknights, weekends, and vacations on this project.

# APPENDIX

# A CONCISE ROADMAP
# TO BUILDING A PMO

As many small companies out there grow, there comes a point when they realize they need to get serious about program management. They may have no program management at all, or there may be a few program managers masquerading as project managers floating around the company—they just don't know it. That's when people often ask me how I built the PMO at Zendesk from the ground up.

These steps for building a PMO have worked for me and resonated with company executives/owners and program management leaders I've advised over the years. Building a PMO isn't a linear exercise, so you may do these steps in a slightly different order depending on your company's infrastructure and resources. Likely you will backtrack and revisit a few steps along your unique journey. Included beneath each step are page references to subsections in the book so you can locate more details on the topics most relevant to your company's situation.

Once your PMO has a few successes under its belt, you'll find that other organizations around the company will ask for PMO support. These requests are a good indication that the work you're doing is having a positive impact and supporting the company's long-term strategy.

Follow this roadmap, and sprinkle in some common sense specific to your situation, and I guarantee the results will make you, your team of program managers, and the company happy. Buckle up and enjoy the journey!

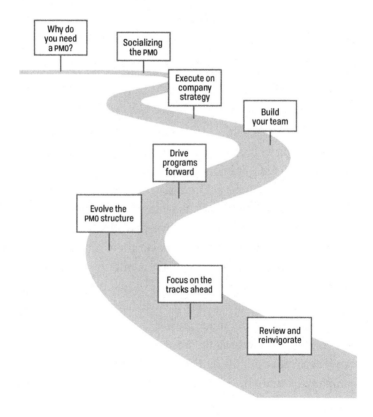

## 1.   Why Do You Need a PMO?

The first step is to answer why the company wants a PMO. Most often it is because they want to drive forward complex, cross-functional programs that support the company's long-term strategy. Next, determine and define your methodology. For example, assuming you are doing strategic execution, draw a diagram and document the process of how the PMO will execute on the company's strategy. A simple diagram might look something like this:

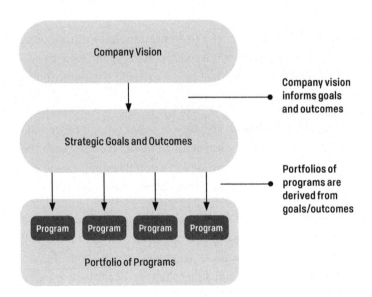

This serves as the foundation for your program management practice. Include this in the slide presentation that you use to socialize the work you're doing and include it in your program management onboarding.

*Chapter One: What Is Program Management?* (p. 11)

*Program Management Onboarding* (p. 177)

## 2. Socialize the PMO

It's imperative to talk about the PMO with stakeholders and team members right from the start so that everyone understands its purpose and what program managers do. You should continually socialize the PMO, particularly as it grows. Branding the PMO is absolutely crucial to this process.

- **Brand the PMO:** Create a presentation that outlines what program management is, who's on the team, how you do your work, and how the business should engage with program managers.

- **Talk about the brand:** Visit the company's major offices and share your presentation at an all hands meeting with the cross-functional program teams you'll begin running programs for, VPs, and executives above the VP level.

- **Protect the brand:** Once the PMO gains some success, this is the time to lean in, own your brand, and continue to sell it. Consider speaking with your manager and your Human Resources department about the PMO exclusively owning the program manager title.

- **Sell the PMO brand:** As the company continues to grow, new hires come in with their own understanding of what program management is. You and/or your PMO leadership team should continue socializing with each new executive and key company hire. Keep your branding deck up to date and encourage others within the PMO to socialize the organization with the business leads at their level.

## 3. Execute on Company Strategy

Program managers run programs that move the needle on company strategy, so they must understand that strategy and ensure the programs they're driving forward map to that strategy.

- **Set goals: Find out what the goals are for the organization(s) you are supporting.** Then understand how those goals will be measured (for example, the expected outcomes). Do this by asking the organization leader and/or your business leads what they expect to accomplish over the next quarter or two, or over the next year. That will lay the groundwork for the programs that need to be put into place to drive to those outcomes.

- **Identify priorities: Determine how many priorities you and your team can reasonably take on.** If you're just building out your team, consider running just a few of the top priority programs and doing them well so people see the value in what you do. Then as your team grows, you can take on more work as determined by company and organizational priorities.

- **Get invited to the party:** Strategic program management requires that a program manager understand the strategic context for the program they are asked to run. You can only do this if you are brought into early strategy discussions.

- **Strategize for the win:** Strategic execution is what program management is all about. As junior program managers are on a learning curve, they may struggle to understand what it means when they're told they need to be less tactical, more strategic. Be patient. It's a skill that comes with experience.

*Setting Success Measures for a Program* (p. 63)
*Measuring the Impact of Program Management* (p. 67)
*Getting Invited to the Party* (p. 52)
*What It Means to Be Strategic* (p. 196)

## 4. Build Your Team

The time has come to build your dream team, but there are a few things to bear in mind as you launch into staffing your PMO.

- **Look for existing program managers:** The right people may already be in your company. Search for people at the company who are already functioning as program managers on the business side. They may be called project managers, even though they are doing cross-functional program work. If they exist, gather them together into one team and determine your initial organization structure.

- **Identify shared work:** Some product managers or engineering leads may be doing some of your work. Once you hire program managers, you can transition that work to free up those other individuals to do what they're best at doing.

- **Develop a job ladder:** Find out what already exists at the company and/or create one from scratch with guidance from Human Resources. Develop a job architecture that outlines the scope, required skills, expectations, and sphere of influence for each position. This will be the foundation for an effective compensation program. Take your team through them (p. 183) to build excitement and interest in how they can progress either as an individual contributor or as a people manager within the PMO.

- **Hire people:** How many people you are able to hire is based on how your PMO is funded (see Step Six). Headcount may come from a central operations organization, such as the COO, or from each of the organizations you support. There are pros and cons to each model, and a hybrid approach can be effective.

- **Onboarding:** Onboarding new hires is critical to ensuring the success of the PMO. Your onboarding process should include everything you know about program managing at your company, but know that the onboarding curriculum will evolve over time as items are added or retired.

- **Learn the business:** This process should be kickstarted with program managers at the time of their onboarding.

Program managers need a solid understanding of the business for the company overall, as well as the organization they were hired to support (engineering, marketing, or sales, for example), especially as they are expected to build relationships and trust with their key business partners.

- **Build for the future:** Hiring top-notch program managers isn't easy. Weed through the CVs of the box checkers and process mavens to find the people with the right EQ and who possess innate people skills.

## 5. Drive Programs Forward

Once your team is ready to go, you'll begin driving programs forward. Follow these basic rules and your trains will run smoothly!

- **Ask questions first:** Establish how the request for assistance will move the company strategy forward by asking the right questions.

- **Kickoff meetings:** Gather your cross-functional program team together to officially kick off the program and align everyone on the program goals and plan.

- **Clarify roles:** Ensure all program team members know what's expected of them.

- **Align the team:** Before you get too far along in the program, make sure the team is aligned on the specifics of the desired outcomes.

- **Communicate often and accurately:** It is crucial to inform all team members and key stakeholders of program status regularly.

- **Mitigate risks efficiently:** A program manager should mitigate risk daily. If a risk develops into an issue, gather program team members together to close that issue. Issues are a top priority for a program manager.

## 6. Evolve the PMO Structure

As you build out a team, you'll need to determine how the PMO will be structured, and there are a few options available to you. PMOs may grow more organically in one company than in another. Here are key issues to wrap your head around.

- **To centralize or not:** Your PMO may start out centralized, or it may start by supporting one organization and then evolve into a centralized organization as more teams ask for support. As you grow the team, you'll need to determine how to fund the additional headcount. As with centralization, there are several options to consider.

- **Consider building a global PMO:** Many companies today are global and any PMO needs to reflect that reality. As you build out your team to support the various global offices, invariably you'll hire program managers all over the world. You may start with just one program manager per office so make this a good hire—you can't afford mistakes.

## 7. Focus on the Tracks Ahead

As you are driving programs forward, you may run into the following issues. They can happen despite a program manager's best intentions, but time and skill will help you avoid them.

- **Losing objectivity:** Program managers are usually embedded with the teams and organizations they support, particularly if they are funded by that organization. That way they are considered part of the team. But there are pros and cons to this setup that you must be aware of, and losing objectivity is a danger to watch out for.

- **Don't become a crutch:** When people see how effective program management is, they often want more of it. Although it's great to be wanted, look out for people who may try to get you to do their jobs.

- **Take action, not notes:** One of the most common misconceptions is that program managers are in the room to take notes. But driving programs forward doesn't mean writing down what has already happened. It's about keeping your eyes on the tracks ahead.

- **Know when to walk away:** Sometimes an organization isn't ready for program management, or they aren't collaborating fully. Occasionally a program manager may need step away until the organization is ready to engage fully with the PMO.

- **Make meetings count:** A quick way to get your team to start groaning and stop attending your program meetings is if they turn into status meetings. Make sure your meeting attendees are getting value out of the meeting time and that all attendees are participating in a productive way.

- **Check your work:** Clear and accurate program status reports are a key part of ensuring your program is successful. Have a PMO colleague check your work before it goes out. This is a useful practice as it ensures you don't sour a healthy relationship with a program team member by inadvertently throwing them under the bus with an unfortunate choice of words.

*No Taking Sides* (p. 199)
*Program Management as a Crutch* (p. 148)
*No Notes Please!* (p. 138)
*When to Walk Away* (p. 157)
*Are Status Meetings Useful?* (p. 127)
*Running Effective Program Team Meetings* (p. 123)
*The Dreaded Laptop in Meetings* (p. 129)
*A Second Pair of Eyes* (p. 136)

## 8. Review and Reinvigorate

You've made it! Your PMO and program managers are running programs successfully and receiving requests for more work. Now's the time to hone your methodology to ensure you are set up for future success. Explore these steps as you review, refine, and reinvigorate.

- **Run retrospectives:** If your company uses the agile methodology, a retrospective is a fairly common practice at the end of a program. However, running them at key milestones also keeps the trains on track.

- **Get the band together:** Program managers are often the catalyst for assembling global team members for an in-person or virtual gathering to ensure alignment at program kickoff and during longer programs as needed. Gatherings like these can short-circuit risks that are building into serious issues or solve issues more efficiently.

- **Stay in the loop:** A key part of running a program is knowing what's going on at all times so you can proactively mitigate risks before they become issues. This involves running effective meetings, building solid relationships with your program team members, and making sure you are getting out and mingling (in person or virtually) with your team.

- **Create dream teams:** Programs are often large and involve many different organizations. Each workstream for a complex program will often have a program manager assigned to it. Try pairing program managers across organizations to make things run smoothly.

- **Flex your superpowers:** Program managers are objective and influence others to get the work done, but these superpowers need to be exercised and updated continually. It's always helpful to reinvigorate your superpowers through professional development and by taking on programs for other organizations as a challenge.

- **Foster trusting relationships:** You've built great relationships with your stakeholders. Take those relationship to the next level.

- **Get comfortable with ambiguity:** In a rapidly changing world, you won't have the luxury of waiting to start a program until you understand everything it will take for it to be successful. Instead of "ready, aim, fire," it's more like "ready, fire, aim."

- **The end is the means:** A program manager's responsibility for a program doesn't end until the desired outcome has been reached. Sometimes that requires ingenuity and patience.

- **Take a spring break:** The nature of some big hairy programs is that they can take what seems like forever to complete. Dependencies for complex programs can cause delays, but when you take a breather in a program, you can often turn a problem into an opportunity.

# RESOURCES

Cain, Susan. *Quiet: The Power of Introverts in a World That Can't Stop Talking.* New York: Broadway Books, 2013.

Catlin, Karen. *Better Allies: Everyday Actions to Create Inclusive, Engaging Workplaces.* Better Allies Press, 2019.

Cooper, John and Wight, Judy. *Implementing a Buddy System in the Workplace* (conference paper). Newtown Square, PA: Project Management Institute, 2014.

Dweck, Carol. *Mindset: The New Psychology of Success.* New York: Ballantine Books, 2007.

Hunt, Vivian, Yee, Lareina, Prince, Sara, and Dixon-Fyle, Sundiatu. *Delivering through Diversity.* McKinsey & Company, January 2018. www.mckinsey.com/business-functions/organization/our-insights/delivering-through-diversity#

Johnson, Spencer. *Who Moved My Cheese?: An Amazing Way to Deal with Change in Your Work and in Your Life.* New York: Putnam, 1998.

Marcus, Bonnie. "What Does It Take to Keep Women in Tech Companies? Ask Them," *Forbes,* November 18, 2018. www.forbes.com/sites/bonniemarcus/2018/11/18/what-does-it-take-to-keep-women-in-tech-companies-ask-them/#28dfe8054249

Ross, D.W. and Shaltry, P.E. *The New PMI Standard for Portfolio Management.* Paper presented at PMI® Global Congress 2006—EMEA, Madrid, Spain. Newtown Square, PA: Project Management Institute, 2006.

Ross, D.W. and Shaltry, P.E. *The New PMI Standard for Program Management.* Paper presented at PMI® Global Congress 2006—North America, Seattle, WA. Newtown Square, PA: Project Management Institute, 2006.

Scott, Kim. *Radical Candor: Be a Kick-ass Boss without Losing Your Humanity.* New York: St. Martin's Press, 2017.

"What Is Project Management?" Project Management Institute. www.pmi.org/about/learn-about-pmi/what-is-project-management.

Zapata, Dushka, *How to Write a Book (or Tackle Anything You Find Daunting).* Self-pub., 2017.

# INDEX

*Page numbers preceded by F indicate figures and by T indicate tables.*

# ABOUT THE AUTHOR

—o—

PAULA DIELI is a software industry executive who has spent decades building software products in both Silicon Valley and Europe. Her career has encompassed roles in engineering, product management, program management, technical support, and localization. This experience has given her a rich understanding of how software is designed, developed, localized, deployed, and supported—a blend of skill sets that gives her a unique edge in creating and running program management teams.

Paula's educational background includes two bachelor's degrees in computer science and French—skills she combined in her work as a software engineer and manager in France. She also earned an MA in French translation.

Paula created this book for the business leaders she advises who want to build a top-notch PMO and for program managers who want to level up their game. It represents the cumulative experience she has gained in developing the best practices that she still uses today. Paula consults with companies on their PMO journeys and mentors many professionals in the software industry. To find out what Paula's up to, visit her website at pauladieli.com.